D0144483

LOGIA OF
BUSINESS ORGANIZATIONS LAW
FOR PARALEGALS

LOGIA OF
BUSINESS ORGANIZATIONS LAW
FOR PARALEGALS

Rodney D. Chrisman

LOGIA PRESS, LLC

Forest, Virginia
2011

Rodney D. Chrisman, *Logia of Business Organizations Law for Paralegals*
Copyright © 2011 by Rodney D. Chrisman

All Rights Reserved. No part of this publication may be reproduced, stored in a retrieval system, or transmitted in any form or by any means electronic, mechanical, or otherwise, including photocopy, recording, or any information storage and retrieval system now known or to be invented, without prior permission in writing from the author, except as provided by law.

Cover art: Moses, Rembrandt van Rijn, 1659

Printed in the United States of America.

Unless otherwise noted, Scripture quotations are taken from the Authorized Version.

ISBN 13: 978-1-937479-01-5

Published by Logia Press, LLC
Forest, Virginia 24551
info@logiapress.com
First Edition: December 2011

For Heather,
my meet-helper whose worth is far above rubies.

PUBLISHER'S PREFACE

"Logia" is the English transliteration of the Greek word "λόγια," which is translated "oracles." This word is used four times in the New Testament. Stephen uses this word in his famous speech in *Acts* 7:38 when he tells the audience that Moses "received the living oracles ["λόγια"] to give unto us." Paul uses it in *Romans* 3:2 when he notes of the Jews "that unto them were committed the oracles ["λόγια"] of God." Peter uses it when he writes that "[i]f any man speak, let him speak as the oracles ["λόγια"] of God." 1 *Peter* 4:11. Finally, the writer of Hebrews uses logia when he castigates his readers for their becoming dull of hearing and not progressing to being teachers as they ought have been by that time (*Hebrews* 5:12-14). He instead states that they needed someone to teach them "the first principles of the oracles ["λόγια"] of God." *Hebrews* 5:12.

In each of the passages described above, "logia" is used to refer to the authoritative pronouncements of the Lord God, including pronouncements in both the Old and New Testament eras. This word, and the corresponding belief that Scripture contains the authoritative pronouncements or logia of God for all areas of life, inspired the name of the publisher, Logia Press, LLC, and this book, Logia of Business Organizations Law for Paralegals. God has spoken His logia. May his people seek to understand and apply His logia in every sphere of life for His glory alone.

Logia Press, LLC
Forest, VA
December, 2011

AUTHOR'S PREFACE AND ACKNOWLEDGEMENTS

The Purpose of the Book

This book is written to help paralegal students learn to apply the Christian worldview to business organizations law issues. It is certainly not complete. Much more could be said about every topic, and for every topic likely hundreds more could be considered. Thus, the hope is not a comprehensive treatment of the Christian worldview of business organizations law (as laudable as that goal would be.) Rather, this book is written with the more modest goal of exposing the students to the application of the Christian worldview to business organizations law in an interesting way that might equip them to continue the practice of the application of that worldview to other issues that they encounter in their lives. The Bible is authoritative for all things to which it speaks, and it speaks to all things.

The Approach of this Book

With the broad purpose stated, I thought it appropriate to state a word about the approach of the book. One of things that I liked best about law school and the practice of law were the interesting cases. The facts of the cases that one encounters in practice and in law school are often very memorable. The writing of certain judges can also be engaging and fascinating. Therefore, I have chosen to structure this book around a number of carefully chosen cases that raise topics that I want us to think through together. I hope that you find the cases as interesting and enjoyable as I have.[1]

The materials following the cases are designed to help you apply the Christian worldview to the case and related topics. Sometimes I attempt a resolution of a particular issue. Other times I do not (or, perhaps, cannot.) The application of a Biblical worldview to the complex legal issues of our day is, to distort an old saying, a row that only a few

---

[1] Only once do I deviate from this practice. In Chapter 4, due to the nature of the topic, I use instead a law review article.

are hoeing. Since few Christian scholars are working in this area in our time, the task to which we shall set ourselves in this book is made all the harder. But, perhaps as a result of this, any successes that God may grant us to enjoy may be all the sweeter.

Finally, as to the approach, I will also include questions that are meant to further stimulate your thought and possibly provide fodder for discussion. Sometimes these questions may cause us to reconsider items that have long been a part of the American legal and business systems. This can be somewhat uncomfortable. However, we should not shy away from this important work. Nothing, even by long use and custom, can become good if God's word condemns it.

A Word as to Judges, Authors, Cases, and Other Materials Cited

Lawyers cite and argue from authorities. Thus, a critical skill for a lawyer, and indeed any person, to develop is the ability to evaluate, distinguish, critique, and learn from various authorities. To that end, I cite a number of cases written by various judges, and I cite materials written by various authors, some of which I would agree with and some of which I would not.

Hopefully this will not be surprising. If this were a book about constitutional law, I would have you read *Roe v. Wade*. Certainly, writing from a Christian worldview, the fact that I would have you read that case would not cause you to draw the conclusion that I agree with everything in it. (The fact is that I agree with very little in it, and I think it is one of the most despicable opinions ever written.) We would read the case, not because we agree with it, but because we do not and it is a part of the legal (and indeed political) fabric of modern America. Many of the materials and authorities quoted, cited, and used in this book are selected for similar reasons.

Therefore, the inclusion of materials in this book, including the cases, should not be construed as an approval or endorsement of the judge, author, or arguments presented merely because of their inclusion in the text. Further, agreement with a judge or author on one point should not be construed as an endorsement of that author on all points. Rather, discernment is needed—and, in my opinion, required. You may not agree with me on all points, and likely you will not. Nor would I likely agree with you on all points. We should be able to state our arguments clearly and even forcefully to one another, and yet remain friends or colleagues. It seems to me that "love your neighbor" requires in this setting that we deal fairly with each argument offered, noting areas of agreement and disagreement, in a professional manner. Further, we should extend that same respect and love to the authors and judges whose materials are contained herein.

Perhaps another quick example will suffice. Included herein is a dissenting opinion by Justice Louis Brandies. I thoroughly disagree with Justice Brandies' approach to jurisprudence, which is merely an extension of his worldview with which I would also thoroughly and strongly disagree. Many of his opinions, and much of his reasoning, I would find reprehensible and destructive for society. However, I still included his dissent in *Louis K. Liggett Co. v. Lee* because it presents arguments regarding the dangers of corporations that need to be thought through from a Christian worldview, not just a secular humanist one. Including his dissent in this case in no way endorses the opinion, Mr. Justice Brandies, nor his approach to life and the law. However, the inclusion does indicate that he raises issues about which Christians should be thinking.

My Approach in Editing of Cases

I have edited the cases contained in this book. If you look these cases up in their full glory, you will likely want to write me and thank me for this. Cases, particularly U.S. Supreme Court cases, tend to be bloated with argumentation and citations that are tedious even for lawyers to read. In fact, many modern Supreme Court cases seemed designed to weary the reader into submission as opposed to winning him over with persuasive argument. I have attempted to spare you the ordeal of being wearied by the sheer number of words alone.

Generally, I have followed the normal editing conventions, such as indicating deleted and inserted material. Deleted material I usually indicated with ellipses or ***. Inserted material is set apart in brackets. Footnotes are often deleted without any indication, as are most citations to other authorities. When footnotes are included, they are typically renumbered in conformity with the numbering used in the book. At times minor corrections, additions, and changes have been made without any indication whatsoever. Further, many grammatical and some spelling errors are left in the cases as they appear in the originals. Language changes over time, and court opinions are no exceptions. Of course, if you have questions about what has been deleted or added, I would direct you to the actual opinions for comparison, as they are freely available from a number of sources on the Internet.

Acknowledgments and Thanks

I would like to thank my lovely bride, Heather, for her love, companionship, support, and editing assistance.

I would also like to thank Dean Jeffrey S. Tuomala for his permission to quote extensively from his excellent article, Marbury v.

Madison *and the Foundation of Law*, 4 LIBERTY U.L. REV. 297, 329-330 (2010).

Obviously, all the mistakes, whether grammatical, typographical, conceptual, or otherwise, remain my own.

And, last but not least, I thank you for reading and studying the book. I hope you grow in your understanding of and love for the law and, more importantly, the Lord who created it.

Soli Deo Gloria

Rodney D. Chrisman
Forest, VA
December, 2011

TABLE OF CONTENTS

CHAPTER 1
AGENCY FORMATION AND REASONING FROM GENERALS TO PARTICULARS

A. Gay Jenson Farms Co. v. Cargill, Inc.
309 N.W.2d 285 (Minn. 1981)

Plaintiffs, 86 individual, partnership or corporate farmers, brought this action against defendant Cargill, Inc. (Cargill) and defendant Warren Grain & Seed Co. (Warren) to recover losses sustained when Warren defaulted on the contracts made with plaintiffs for the sale of grain. After a trial by jury, judgment was entered in favor of plaintiffs, and Cargill brought this appeal. We affirm.

This case arose out of the financial collapse of defendant Warren Seed & Grain Co., and its failure to satisfy its indebtedness to plaintiffs. Warren, which was located in Warren, Minnesota, was operated by Lloyd Hill and his son, Gary Hill. Warren operated a grain elevator and as a result was involved in the purchase of cash or market grain from local farmers. The cash grain would be resold through the Minneapolis Grain Exchange or to the terminal grain companies directly. Warren also stored grain for farmers and sold chemicals, fertilizer and steel storage bins. In addition, it operated a seed business which involved buying seed grain from farmers, processing it and reselling it for seed to farmers and local elevators.

Lloyd Hill decided in 1964 to apply for financing from Cargill. Cargill's officials from the Moorhead regional office investigated Warren's operations and recommended that Cargill finance Warren.

Warren and Cargill thereafter entered into a security agreement which provided that Cargill would loan money for working capital to Warren on "open account" financing up to a stated limit, which was originally set as $175,000. Under this contract, Warren would receive funds and pay its expenses by issuing drafts drawn on Cargill through Minneapolis banks. The drafts were imprinted with both Warren's and

Cargill's names. Proceeds from Warren's sales would be deposited with Cargill and credited to its account. In return for this financing, Warren appointed Cargill as its grain agent for transaction with the Commodity Credit Corporation. Cargill was also given a right of first refusal to purchase market grain sold by Warren to the terminal market.

A new contract was negotiated in 1967, extending Warren's credit line to $300,000 and incorporating the provisions of the original contract. It was also stated in the contract that Warren would provide Cargill with annual financial statements and that either Cargill would keep the books for Warren or an audit would be conducted by an independent firm. Cargill was given the right of access to Warren's books for inspection.

In addition, the agreement provided that Warren was not to make capital improvements or repairs in excess of $5,000 without Cargill's prior consent. Further, it was not to become liable as guarantor on another's indebtedness, or encumber its assets except with Cargill's permission. Consent by Cargill was required before Warren would be allowed to declare a dividend or sell and purchase stock.

Officials from Cargill's regional office made a brief visit to Warren shortly after the agreement was executed. They examined the annual statement and the accounts receivable, expenses, inventory, seed, machinery and other financial matters. Warren was informed that it would be reminded periodically to make the improvements recommended by Cargill. At approximately this time, a memo was given to the Cargill official in charge of the Warren account, Erhart Becker, which stated in part: "This organization (Warren) needs very strong paternal guidance."

In 1970, Cargill contracted with Warren and other elevators to act as its agent to seek growers for a new type of wheat called Bounty 208. Warren, as Cargill's agent for this project, entered into contracts for the growing of the wheat seed, with Cargill named as the contracting party. Farmers were paid directly by Cargill for the seed and all contracts were performed in full. In 1971, pursuant to an agency contract, Warren contracted on Cargill's behalf with various farmers for the growing of sunflower seeds for Cargill. The arrangements were similar to those made in the Bounty 208 contracts, and all those contracts were also completed. Both these agreements were unrelated to the open account financing contract. In addition, Warren, as Cargill's agent in the sunflower seed business, cleaned and packaged the seed in Cargill bags.

During this period, Cargill continued to review Warren's operations and expenses and recommend that certain actions should be taken. Warren purchased from Cargill various business forms printed by Cargill and received sample forms from Cargill which Warren used to develop its own business forms.

Cargill wrote to its regional office in 1970 expressing its concern that the pattern of increased use of funds allowed to develop at Warren was similar to that involved in two other cases in which Cargill experienced severe losses. Cargill did not refuse to honor drafts or call the loan, however. A new security agreement which increased the credit line to $750,000 was executed in 1972, and a subsequent agreement which raised the limit to $1,250,000 was entered into in 1976.

Warren was at that time shipping Cargill 90% of its cash grain. When Cargill's facilities were full, Warren shipped its grain to other companies. Approximately 25% of Warren's total sales was seed grain which was sold directly by Warren to its customers.

As Warren's indebtedness continued to be in excess of its credit line, Cargill began to contact Warren daily regarding its financial affairs. Cargill headquarters informed its regional office in 1973 that, since Cargill money was being used, Warren should realize that Cargill had the right to make some critical decisions regarding the use of the funds. Cargill headquarters also told Warren that a regional manager would be working with Warren on a day-to-day basis as well as in monthly planning meetings. In 1975, Cargill's regional office began to keep a daily debit position on Warren. A bank account was opened in Warren's name on which Warren could draw checks in 1976. The account was to be funded by drafts drawn on Cargill by the local bank.

In early 1977, it became evident that Warren had serious financial problems. Several farmers, who had heard that Warren's checks were not being paid, inquired or had their agents inquire at Cargill regarding Warren's status and were initially told that there would be no problem with payment. In April 1977, an audit of Warren revealed that Warren was $4 million in debt. After Cargill was informed that Warren's financial statements had been deliberately falsified, Warren's request for additional financing was refused. In the final days of Warren's operation, Cargill sent an official to supervise the elevator, including disbursement of funds and income generated by the elevator.

After Warren ceased operations, it was found to be indebted to Cargill in the amount of $3.6 million. Warren was also determined to be indebted to plaintiffs in the amount of $2 million, and plaintiffs brought this action in 1977 to seek recovery of that sum. Plaintiffs alleged that Cargill was jointly liable for Warren's indebtedness as it had acted as principal for the grain elevator.

The matter was bifurcated for trial in Marshall County District Court. In the first phase, the amount of damages sustained by each farmer was determined by the court. The second phase of the action, dealing with the issue of Cargill's liability for the indebtedness of Warren, was tried before a jury.

The jury found that Cargill's conduct between 1973 and 1977 had made it Warren's principal. Warren was found to be the agent of Cargill with regard to contracts for:

1. The purchase and sale of grain for market.
2. The purchase and sale of seed grain.
3. The storage of grain.

The court determined that Cargill was the disclosed principal of Warren. It was concluded that Cargill was jointly liable with Warren for plaintiffs' losses, and judgment was entered for plaintiffs.

Cargill seeks a reversal of the jury's findings or, if the jury findings are upheld, a reversal of the trial court's determination that Cargill was a disclosed principal. In the alternative, Cargill requests that the court order a new trial based upon the trial court's error in (1) denying Cargill's requested jury instructions; (2) refusing to admit relevant evidence; and (3) denying Cargill's motion for change of venue. Northwestern County Elevator Association, North Dakota Grain Dealers Association and Northwestern National Bank of Minneapolis have all filed briefs on appeal as amici curiae, seeking to have the jury verdict reversed.

. . . The major issue in this case is whether Cargill, by its course of dealing with Warren, became liable as a principal on contracts made by Warren with plaintiffs. Cargill contends that no agency relationship was established with Warren, notwithstanding its financing of Warren's operation and its purchase of the majority of Warren's grain. However, we conclude that Cargill, by its control and influence over Warren, became a principal with liability for the transactions entered into by its agent Warren.

Agency is the fiduciary relationship that results from the manifestation of consent by one person to another that the other shall act on his behalf and subject to his control, and consent by the other so to act. . . . RESTATEMENT (SECOND) OF AGENCY § 1 (1958). In order to create an agency there must be an agreement, but not necessarily a contract between the parties. RESTATEMENT (SECOND) OF AGENCY § 1, cmt. b (1958). An agreement may result in the creation of an agency relationship although the parties did not call it an agency and did not intend the legal consequences of the relation to follow. *Id.* The existence of the agency may be proved by circumstantial evidence which shows a course of dealing between the two parties. . . . When an agency relationship is to be proven by circumstantial evidence, the principal must be shown to have consented to the agency since one cannot be the agent of another except by consent of the latter. . . .

Cargill contends that the prerequisites of an agency relationship did not exist because Cargill never consented to the agency, Warren did not act on behalf of Cargill, and Cargill did not exercise control over Warren. We hold that all three elements of agency could be found in the particular circumstances of this case. By directing Warren to implement its recommendations, Cargill manifested its consent that Warren would be its agent. Warren acted on Cargill's behalf in procuring grain for Cargill as the part of its normal operations which were totally financed by Cargill. Further, an agency relationship was established by Cargill's interference with the internal affairs of Warren, which constituted de facto control of the elevator.

A creditor who assumes control of his debtor's business may become liable as principal for the acts of the debtor in connection with the business. RESTATEMENT (SECOND) OF AGENCY § 14O (1958). It is noted in comment a to Section 14O that:

> A security holder who merely exercises a veto power over the business acts of his debtor by preventing purchases or sales above specified amounts does not thereby become a principal. However, if he takes over the management of the debtor's business either in person or through an agent, and directs what contracts may or may not be made, he becomes a principal, liable as a principal for the obligations incurred thereafter in the normal course of business by the debtor who has now become his general agent. The point at which the creditor becomes a principal is that at which he assumes de facto control over the conduct of his debtor, whatever the terms of the formal contract with his debtor may be.

A number of factors indicate Cargill's control over Warren, including the following:

(1) Cargill's constant recommendations to Warren by telephone;

(2) Cargill's right of first refusal on grain;

(3) Warren's inability to enter into mortgages, to purchase stock or to pay dividends without Cargill's approval;

(4) Cargill's right of entry onto Warren's premises to carry on periodic checks and audits;

(5) Cargill's correspondence and criticism regarding Warren's finances, officers salaries and inventory;

(6) Cargill's determination that Warren needed "strong paternal guidance";

(7) Provision of drafts and forms to Warren upon which Cargill's name was imprinted;

(8) Financing of all Warren's purchases of grain and operating expenses; and

(9) Cargill's power to discontinue the financing of Warren's operations.

We recognize that some of these elements, as Cargill contends, are found in an ordinary debtor-creditor relationship. However, these factors cannot be considered in isolation, but, rather, they must be viewed in light of all the circumstances surrounding Cargill's aggressive financing of Warren.

It is also Cargill's position that the relationship between Cargill and Warren was that of buyer-supplier rather than principal-agent. RESTATEMENT (SECOND) OF AGENCY § 14K (1958) compares an agent with a supplier as follows:

> One who contracts to acquire property from a third person and convey it to another is the agent of the other only if it is agreed that he is to act primarily for the benefit of the other and not for himself.

Factors indicating that one is a supplier, rather than an agent, are:

> (1) That he is to receive a fixed price for the property irrespective of price paid by him. This is the most important. (2) That he acts in his own name and receives the title to the property which he thereafter is to transfer. (3) That he has an independent business in buying and selling similar property.

RESTATEMENT (SECOND) OF AGENCY § 14K, CMT. A (1958).

Under the Restatement approach, it must be shown that the supplier has an independent business before it can be concluded that he is not an agent. The record establishes that all portions of Warren's operation were financed by Cargill and that Warren sold almost all of its market grain to Cargill. Thus, the relationship which existed between the parties was not merely that of buyer and supplier.

. . .

Further, we are not persuaded by the fact that Warren was not one of the "line" elevators that Cargill operated in its own name. The Warren operation, like the line elevator, was financially dependent on Cargill's continual infusion of capital. The arrangement with Warren presented a convenient alternative to the establishment of a line elevator. Cargill became, in essence, the owner of the operation without the accompanying legal indicia.

The amici curiae assert that, if the jury verdict is upheld, firms and banks which have provided business loans to county elevators will decline to make further loans. The decision in this case should give no cause for such concern. We deal here with a business enterprise markedly different from an ordinary bank financing, since Cargill was an active participant in Warren's operations rather than simply a financier. Cargill's course of dealing with Warren was, by its own admission, a paternalistic relationship in which Cargill made the key economic decisions and kept Warren in existence.

Although considerable interest was paid by Warren on the loan, the reason for Cargill's financing of Warren was not to make money as a lender but, rather, to establish a source of market grain for its business. As one Cargill manager noted, "We were staying in there because we wanted the grain." For this reason, Cargill was willing to extend the credit line far beyond the amount originally allocated to Warren. It is noteworthy that Cargill was receiving significant amounts of grain and that, notwithstanding the risk that was recognized by Cargill, the operation was considered profitable.

On the whole, there was a unique fabric in the relationship between Cargill and Warren which varies from that found in normal debtor-creditor situations. We conclude that, on the facts of this case, there was sufficient evidence from which the jury could find that Cargill was the principal of Warren within the definitions of agency set forth in RESTATEMENT (SECOND) OF AGENCY §§ 1 AND 140.

. . .

Finally, Cargill claims that the trial court's denial of its motion for a change of venue was improper. Cargill moved for a change of venue pursuant to Minn.Stat. s 542.11 (1980), because it was not satisfied with the impartiality of the jury. Section 542.11 permits the trial court to exercise its discretion in determining when a change of venue is appropriate.

. . .

Cargill's motion was made during the jury selection process. On group examination, 26 of the 60 veniremen were excused for cause, either because of relationship to the parties or because of prejudice. Of the 14 jurors who were seated, 2 were excused for cause. Several of the jurors said that they had information concerning the case. The trial court noted that all 14 jurors, including the 2 excused for cause, said that they would lay aside their impressions and opinions and render a fair and impartial decision.

The mere fact that the jury had knowledge of the financial collapse of Warren and its connection with Cargill does not indicate that it could not render a fair decision. Further, Cargill had 13 months from the filing of the lawsuit to commencement of the trial to ascertain that Warren was a small community and that jurors from that area could be presumed to have some association with the elevator or with one of the 86 plaintiffs. Also, Cargill's counsel, as well as plaintiffs' counsel, referred to the economic impact of the decision on the community. Thus, the trial court's denial of a change of venue was a proper exercise of discretion.

Affirmed.

NOTES AND QUESTIONS

1. Reasoning from Generals to Particulars. The issue of the relationship of generals to particulars has plagued philosophers for millennia. It is at least as old as Plato and Aristotle. In fact, the famous painting by the Italian Renaissance artist Raphael called the School of Athens is meant to capture this debate. Plato in the fresco is pointing up in reference to the general principles (or forms as Plato understood them) being the most important thing while Aristotle is portrayed with his hand down indicating that reality actually resides most ultimately in the various particulars.

Despite the many attempts throughout the years by philosophers holding various worldviews, it is only within a Christian worldview that this issue can be satisfactorily resolved. In fact, only within a Christian worldview do we have any reason to believe that there would be any relationship between the generals and particulars at all.[1]

In a naturalistic evolutionary worldview, where everything is simply governed by time and chance operating upon matter (and chaos is therefore king,) why would one expect there to be any relationship between generals and particulars? Why would one expect to see order? Why would one have reason to believe that what has happened in the past is in any way indicative of what will happen in the future?

Indeed, many non-Christian thinkers have come to this conclusion. Generally, they have decided to live as if what they believe is not true and assume that there is a reason to expect order in the world. They have generally sought a connection between generals and particulars, even though their worldviews tell them there should be none.

In the Christian worldview, we have every reason to believe that generals and particulars relate because a sovereign and loving Lord created the universe and sustains it still. *See Colossians* 1:17 and *Hebrews* 1:3 (Christ is even now "upholding all things by the word of his power"). Therefore, the order in the universe comes from the Creator. We should expect to be able to discover this order and guiding principles within this order (generals or universals) and then be able to rationally apply these generals to various situations (particulars.)

Let's take an example from the Scriptures. In answer a question posed to Him, Jesus said, in *Matthew* 22:37-40, that:

> Thou shalt love the Lord thy God with all thy heart, and with
> all thy soul, and with all thy mind. This is the first and great

---

[1] Or, for that matter, between the particulars themselves. The particulars could just be random, unconnected, chaotic events. In fact, it would be fair to ask, from an evolutionary point of view, why one would expect to see any order or meaning in the world at all.

> commandment. And the second is like unto it, Thou shalt
> love thy neighbour as thyself. On these two commandments
> hang all the law and the prophets.

It is important to note that Jesus does not stop with the statement of the two greatest commandments (presumably therefore the two greatest general principles,) but He goes on to assert that on these two commandments all of the rest of Scripture hangs.

Thus, upon hearing that "love God" is the greatest commandment, one might ask, "how do I love God?" Without Jesus' second assertion, this might be very difficult to answer. But, applying Jesus' words, it becomes much easier to answer. Why? Because the Bible gives us not only general principles but more particular applications of those principles as well. Accordingly, as we look into the Bible to find how we should love God, we find that one way to love Him is to have no other God's before Him. Another way is to make no graven images or idols. In addition, one loves God by not using His name in vain. God is also loved when we honor the Sabbath day and keep it holy. *See Exodus* 20:1-8; *Deuteronomy* 6:5 and 5:6-12.

You have probably already noticed that the above list contains the first four of the Ten Commandments, which are often referred to as the first table of the law. We can do the same thing with the last six of the Ten Commandments, or the second table of the law.

How do I love my neighbor as myself? One way is to honor my father and mother. Other ways include not committing murder, adultery, or theft. Also, if I want to love my neighbor, I should not bear false witness against him nor covet anything that God has entrusted to him. *See Leviticus* 19:18; *Exodus* 20:9-17; and *Deuteronomy* 5:13-21.

As you can see, we are moving from broad general principles (i.e., love God) to more specific application of those principles (i.e., don't commit adultery.) And, of course, we need not stop there. There are increasing levels of specificity contained within the Scriptures. For instance, one might inquire as to the meaning of "do not commit adultery." Is that limited to sexual intercourse with someone to whom one is not married only?

In the Sermon on the Mount, Jesus answers this question in the negative. He asserts that the actual general rule is much broader than that. He states that "do not commit adultery" includes also not lusting after a woman in your heart. Thus, we might state this chain of moving from generality to increasing particularity in this way: one of the ways in which one should love his neighbor is by exercising and demonstrating sexual purity. Sexual purity includes not committing the physical act of adultery, but it also goes much further, even to the point of including the specific command that he should not even lust after his neighbor's wife.[2]

Reasoning from generality to specificity, as we have been doing above, is a biblical way of thinking, and it only makes sense in a Christian worldview where order can be expected in the world. As noted earlier, because God is the Creator and Sustainer of the world, we can expect to find order and relationship in the world. Thus, reasoning from generality to particularity is possible.

The issue of the discerning of generals or universals and their relationship and application to particulars is foundational to the practice of law. In the Western legal tradition, much of the work of law consists of identifying general rules and principles and applying those generals to various specific situations.

Virtually every area of law contains general rules that are applied to specific cases by judges and juries.[3] To help illustrate this, let's consider a general rule from the law of agency, which was at issue in *Cargill*.

An initial question that often needs to be answered in cases dealing with agency matters is whether an agency relationship exists at all. Over the centuries, the common law has developed general principles (or rules) for determining when an agency relationship exists. Like the court in *Cargill*, let's use the RESTATEMENT OF THE LAW (SECOND) AGENCY for the wording of the general rules that we will consider. In one relevant portion, it reads as follows:

> (1) Agency is the fiduciary relation which results from the manifestation of consent by one person to another that the other shall act on his behalf and subject to his control, and consent by the other so to act.
> (2) The one for whom action is to be taken is the principal.
> (3) The one who is to act is the agent.

RESTATEMENT (SECOND) OF AGENCY § 1 (1958).

Restating this general rule as a test, an agency relationship results when the principal manifests consent that the agent shall (1) act on the

---

[2] Note that by not lusting after other women, a man is also loving his wife (or future wife, as the case may be.) Obviously, the reverse could be stated from the female perspective and it would be equally valid.

[3] Does this also apply to legislatures such as the United States Congress? Unfortunately, we do not often think of it in quite this way, but we should. Congress should be attempting to pass specific pieces of legislation (particulars) that are in accord with the principles upon which God has built the world. For example, in earlier eras, if a bill was proposed in Congress, the proponent of the bill might expect to be asked where he found support for such an idea in the Bible. Regrettably, such a discussion is unimaginable today.

principal's behalf and (2) act subject to the principal's control, and (3) the agent manifests consent to so act (i.e., on the principal's behalf and subject to the principal's control.) If this test is satisfied, then the law will recognize an agency relationship. As the *Cargill* case demonstrates, certain results follow from the conclusion that a principal-agent relationship exists, such as the ability of the agent to bind the principal in contract.

Looking at this general rule, did the *Cargill* court apply this rule correctly? Or, was the court actually applying a different rule? If so, what is that rule and did the court apply it correctly? What do you think that outcome should have been based upon the general rule set forth above? What do you think would be a just outcome? Are they the same?

_____

_____

_____

_____

_____

_____

2. Commentators on **Cargill.** Commentators tend to agree that the *Cargill* opinion is not a good example of sound judicial reasoning. For example, the RESTATEMENT OF THE LAW (THIRD) AGENCY (2006) in the Reporter's Notes (f)(1) to § 1.01, states that "Control, however defined, is by itself insufficient to establish agency. In the debtor-creditor context, most courts are reluctant to find relationships of agency on the basis of provisions in agreements that protect the creditor's interests. . . . An unusual example to the contrary is [*Cargill*]."

Prof. Hynes also found the reasoning of the *Cargill* court unpersuasive. His comments on the portion of the opinion addressing the requirement that a principal manifest consent that the agent act on his behalf and the agent consents so to act are illustrative. He writes:

> The court also addressed the "on behalf of" element in agency law, stating "Warren acted on Cargill's behalf in procuring grain for Cargill as the part of its normal operations which were totally financed by Cargill." This analysis is factually unsound. It overlooks the fact that Warren made a profit on its sales of grain to Cargill. The profit was not shared with Cargill. The court does not address this point, but the language of the briefs on both sides of this case makes it clear Warren *sold* grain to Cargill and did not *procure* grain for Cargill.

In support of satisfaction of the "on behalf of" element, plaintiffs argued the action of selling grain to Cargill benefitted Cargill because Warren earned income through which it could pay off its loan to Cargill. This is unquestionably true. But doesn't the argument prove too much? It equates receiving payments under a loan with receiving profits from a business. It transposes actions that benefit another into actions on behalf of another through mere recitation of the fact of benefit. It carries strict liability well beyond the foundations of traditional agency law.

It is true that Cargill was the primary lender to Warren, that the loans were substantial in nature and appeared to be essential to the ongoing operation of the business. The court mentioned Cargill's "aggressive financing" of Warren and noted Cargill had the "power to discontinue the financing of Warren's operations." This is not uncommon in debtor-creditor business relationships. Of what legal significance, however, is it that one creditor is so important to a business? Surely that fact alone cannot fairly support an inference that the debtor's business is being run on the creditor's behalf. Instead, it serves only as a basis for inferring control.

J. Dennis Hynes, *Lender Liability: The Dilemma of the Controlling Creditor*, 58 TENN. L. REV. 635, 653-654 (1991) (footnotes omitted).

Finally, Prof. Kleinberger argues that the opinion should be thought of as an example of "constructive agency" (a term of Prof. Kleinberger's creation) instead of actual or true agency. DANIEL S. KLEINBERGER, EXAMPLES AND EXPLANATIONS § 6.3 (2008). "The Cargill case is troubling both conceptually and practically. The court tries to justify its decision under R.2d, section 1, as well as under section 14 O, and thereby confuses constructive agency with true agency." *Id.* Further, Prof. Kleinberger rejects the court's assertions that this case involves something wholly distinct from the normal debtor-creditor relationship. He concludes that "the Cargill court's attempt to distinguish the Cargill-Warren situation from normal debtor-creditor relationships is unpersuasive." *Id.* Is Prof. Kleinberger right? Can you distinguish this case from a local bank that does inventory and customer financing for a car dealership? Or, do creditors have reason for concern, despite what the court in *Cargill* says?

_____

_____

_____

_____

_____

_____

3. An Outcome-Based Decision? In law there is an old saw that says: "bad facts make bad law." In other words, bad or sympathetic facts can often lead to judges (and juries) straining a general principle to reach a desired outcome in a given factual situation. While this type of outcome-based reasoning is tempting for obvious reasons, it undermines the rule of law by failing to reason properly from generals to particulars and therefore should be resisted.

Could the *Cargill* case be an example of outcome-based reasoning as opposed to proper reasoning from generals to particulars? As noted above, most commentators conclude that the court is not reasoning correctly from the general rules of agency law to the particulars of the case. Could it be that the outcome was determined more because the case arose during the so-called "Great Grain Robbery" and it was tried in the Midwest in a small farming community? Is that justice? *See Exodus* 23:1-9; *Leviticus* 19:15; and *Deuteronomy* 1:16-17.

_____

_____

_____

_____

_____

_____

4. Impact Upon the Rule of Law. The United States government and the governments of the various states are supposed to be governments of laws, not men. *Lex rex,* or "the law is king." This means that the law governs all people and should be stated in principles and rules that are applied in a similar fashion to those similarly situated. In other words, the America system is based upon what is often called the rule of law.

Opinions like *Cargill* undermine the rule of law. Perhaps, in reading the opinion, one might feel that Cargill should be made to answer for the debts of Warren. While one might feel this way, in a rule-of-law society, liability should not be imposed upon a party without an adequate basis in law for doing so. Thus, even if one finds the outcome of *Cargill* satisfying, the outcome-based reasoning of the case typifies a rejection of the rule of law that is ultimately dangerous to justice and liberty in our society.

CHAPTER 2
SCOPE OF EMPLOYMENT AND JUDICIAL V. PRUDENTIAL REASONING

Ira S. Bushey & Sons, Inc. v. United States
398 F.2d 167 (2d Cir. 1968)

FRIENDLY, J. While the United States Coast Guard vessel Tamaroa was being overhauled in a floating drydock located in Brooklyn's Gowanus Canal, a seaman returning from shore leave late at night, in the condition for which seamen are famed, turned some wheels on the drydock wall. He thus opened valves that controlled the flooding of the tanks on one side of the drydock. Soon the ship listed, slid off the blocks and fell against the wall. Parts of the drydock sank, and the ship partially did—fortunately without loss of life or personal injury. The drydock owner sought and was granted compensation by the District Court for the Eastern District of New York in an amount to be determined, . . . ; the United States appeals.

. . .

. . . The Tamaroa had gone into drydock on February 28, 1963; her keel rested on blocks permitting her drive shaft to be removed and repairs to be made to her hull. The contract between the Government and Bushey provided in part:

(o) The work shall, whenever practical, be performed in such manner as not to interfere with the berthing and messing of personnel attached to the vessel undergoing repair, and provision shall be made so that personnel assigned shall have access to the vessel at all times, it being understood that such personnel will not interfere with the work or the contractor's workmen.

Access from shore to ship was provided by a route past the security guard at the gate, through the yard, up a ladder to the top of one drydock wall and along the wall to a gangway leading to the fantail deck, where men returning from leave reported at a quartermaster's shack.

Seaman Lane, whose prior record was unblemished, returned from shore leave a little after midnight on March 14. He had been drinking heavily; the quartermaster made mental note that he was "loose." For reasons not apparent to us or very likely to Lane [who disappeared after completing the sentence imposed by the court-martial and being discharged], he took it into his head, while progressing along the gangway wall, to turn each of three large wheels some twenty times; unhappily, as previously stated, these wheels controlled the water intake valves. After boarding ship at 12:11 A.M., Lane mumbled to an off-duty seaman that he had 'turned some valves' and also muttered something about 'valves' to another who was standing the engineering watch. Neither did anything; apparently Lane's condition was not such as to encourage proximity. At 12:20 A.M. a crew member discovered water coming into the drydock. By 12:30 A.M. the ship began to list, the alarm was sounded and the crew were ordered ashore. Ten minutes later the vessel and dock were listing over 20 degrees; in another ten minutes the ship slid off the blocks and fell against the drydock wall.

The Government attacks imposition of liability on the ground that Lane's acts were not within the scope of his employment. It relies heavily on § 228(1) of the RESTATEMENT OF AGENCY 2D which says that "conduct of a servant is within the scope of employment if, but only if: * * * (c) it is actuated, at least in part by a purpose to serve the master." Courts have gone to considerable lengths to find such a purpose, as witness a well-known opinion in which Judge Learned Hand concluded that a drunken boatswain who routed the plaintiff out of his bunk with a blow, saying "Get up, you big son of a bitch, and turn to," and then continued to fight, might have thought he was acting in the interest of the ship. *Nelson v. American-West African Line*, 86 F.2d 730 (2 Cir. 1936), *cert. denied*, 300 U.S. 665, 57 S.Ct. 509, 81 L.Ed. 873 (1937). It would be going too far to find such a purpose here; while Lane's return to the Tamaroa was to serve his employer, no one has suggested how he could have thought turning the wheels to be, even if—which is by no means clear—he was unaware of the consequences.

In light of the highly artificial way in which the motive test has been applied, the district judge believed himself obliged to test the doctrine's continuing vitality by referring to the larger purposes *respondeat superior* is supposed to serve. He concluded that the old formulation failed this test. We do not find his analysis so compelling, however, as to constitute a sufficient basis in itself for discarding the old doctrine. It is not at all clear, as the court below suggested, that expansion of liability in the manner here suggested will lead to a more efficient allocation of resources. As the most astute exponent of this theory has emphasized, a more efficient allocation can only be expected if there is some reason to believe that imposing a particular cost on the enterprise will lead it to consider whether steps should be taken to prevent a recurrence of the accident. . . . And the suggestion that imposition of liability here will lead to more intensive screening of employees rests on highly questionable premises . . . . The unsatisfactory quality of the allocation of resource rationale is especially striking on the facts of this case. It could well be that application of the traditional rule might induce drydock owners, prodded by their insurance companies, to install locks on their valves to avoid similar incidents in the future, while placing the burden on shipowners is much less likely to lead to accident prevention. It is true, of course, that in many cases the plaintiff will not be in a position to insure, and so expansion of liability will, at the very least, serve *respondeat superior's* loss spreading function. . . . But the fact that the defendant is better able to afford damages is not alone sufficient to justify legal responsibility, . . . and this overarching principle must be taken into account in deciding whether to expand the reach of respondeat superior.

A policy analysis thus is not sufficient to justify this proposed expansion of vicarious liability. This is not surprising since *respondeat superior*, even within its traditional limits, rests not so much on policy grounds consistent with the governing principles of tort law as in a deeply rooted sentiment that a business enterprise cannot justly disclaim responsibility for accidents which may fairly be said to be characteristic of its activities. It is in this light that the inadequacy of the motive test becomes apparent. Whatever may have been the case in the past, a doctrine that would create such drastically different consequences for the actions of the drunken boatswain in Nelson and those of the drunken seaman here reflects a wholly unrealistic attitude toward the risks characteristically attendant upon the operation of a ship. We concur in the statement of Mr. Justice Rutledge in a case involving violence injuring a fellow-worker, in this instance in the context of workmen's compensation:

> Men do not discard their personal qualities when they go to work. Into the job they carry their intelligence, skill, habits of care and rectitude. Just as inevitably they take along also their tendencies to carelessness and camaraderie, as well as emotional make-up. In bringing men together, work brings

these qualities together, causes frictions between them, creates occasions for lapses into carelessness, and for fun-making and emotional flare-up. * * * These expressions of human nature are incidents inseparable from working together. The involve risks of injury and these risks are inherent in the working environment.

Hartford Accident & Indemnity Co. v. Cardillo, 72 App.D.C. 52, 112 F.2d 11, 15, *cert. denied*, 310 U.S. 649, 60 S.Ct. 1100, 84 L.Ed. 1415 (1940). . . . Put another way, Lane's conduct was not so "unforeseeable" as to make it unfair to charge the Government with responsibility. We agree with a leading treatise that

> what is reasonably foreseeable in this context (of *respondeat superior*) * * * is quite a different thing from the foreseeably unreasonable risk of harm that spells negligence * * *. The foresight that should impel the prudent man to take precautions is not the same measure as that by which he should perceive the harm likely to flow from his long-run activity in spite of all reasonable precautions on his own part. The proper test here bears far more resemblance to that which limits liability for workmen's compensation than to the test for negligence. The employer should be held to expect risks, to the public also, which arise "out of and in the course of" his employment of labor.

2 HARPER & JAMES, THE LAW OF TORTS 1377-78 (1956). . . . Here it was foreseeable that crew members crossing the drydock might do damage, negligently or even intentionally, such as pushing a Bushey employee or kicking property into the water. Moreover, the proclivity of seamen to find solace for solitude by copious resort to the bottle while ashore has been noted in opinions too numerous to warrant citation. Once all this is granted, it is immaterial that Lane's precise action was not to be foreseen. . . . Consequently, we can no longer accept our past decisions that have refused to move beyond the Nelson rule . . . since they do not accord with modern understanding as to when it is fair for an enterprise to disclaim the actions of its employees.

One can readily think of cases that fall on the other side of the line. If Lane had set fire to the bar where he had been imbibing or had caused an accident on the street while returning to the drydock, the Government would not be liable; the activities of the 'enterprise' do not reach into areas where the servant does not create risks different from those attendant on the activities of the community in general. . . . We agree with the district judge that if the seaman "upon returning to the drydock, recognized the

Bushey security guard as his wife's lover and shot him," . . . vicarious liability would not follow; the incident would have related to the seaman's domestic life, not to his seafaring activity, . . . and it would have been the most unlikely happenstance that the confrontation with the paramour occurred on a drydock rather than at the traditional spot. Here Lane had come within the closed-off area where his ship lay . . . to occupy a berth to which the Government insisted he have access, . . . and while his act is not readily explicable, at least it was not shown to be due entirely to facets of his personal life. The risk that seamen going and coming from the Tamaroa might cause damage to the drydock is enough to make it fair that the enterprise bear the loss. It is not a fatal objection that the rule we lay down lacks sharp contours; in the end, as Judge Andrews said in a related context, "it is all a question (of expediency,) * * * of fair judgment, always keeping in mind the fact that we endeavor to make a rule in each case that will be practical and in keeping with the general understanding of Mankind." *Palsgraf v. Long Island R.R. Co.*,248 N.Y. 339, 354-355, 162 N.E. 99, 104, 59 A.L.R. 1253 (1928) (dissenting opinion).

        . . .

Affirmed.

NOTES AND QUESTIONS

1. Judicial v. Prudential Reasoning. In the previous chapter, we saw that the relationship of generals to particulars is foundational to American law, including the law of business organizations. In this chapter, we will consider another foundational idea in American law: the contrast between judicial and prudential reasoning. Like the issue of general and particulars, the concept of judicial v. prudential reasoning also impacts the law of business organizations.

The American constitutional system includes as one of its core principles the idea that liberty is best ensured in a system that includes a robust separation of powers. Separation of powers is simply the idea that the powers of government should be separated into various departments or institutions. In our system this includes a separation between the judicial branch and the legislative branch.

This idea is based upon a solid biblical foundation. While the prevailing secular humanist worldview understands man to be essentially good and perfectable, the biblical worldview understands man's fallen condition. Fallen men are prone to selfishness and evil, and we all struggle to act altruistically. To paraphrase the Federalist Papers, men are not angels. *See, e.g., Genesis* 3 and *Romans* 3:9-23.

Since men are not angels, a separation of powers works to limit the consolidation of power in any one person or institution. By limiting the power any one person or institution can wield, freedom is better preserved.

Most Americans wholeheartedly support the idea of a separation of powers within our system. Generally, we as a people are very proud of our Constitutional system and its features. However, unfortunately, our understanding of what these principles actually mean has greatly diminished, even among those who should know better.

One such striking example related to this issue is the difference between political and judicial powers, roles, and decision-making. Judges and the courts are entrusted with judicial power and should engage in judicial reasoning, while the legislature is entrusted with legislative power and should engage in legislative reasoning. Dean Jeffrey S. Tuomala,[1] in his excellent article entitled Marbury v. Madison *and the Foundation of Law*, describes these two types of power and their correlative styles of reasoning as follows:

> The action of legislating, which includes the adoption of a constitution, is forward-looking or prospective in nature. The focus in the legislative process is not upon determining what happened at some particular time in the past in some discrete situation. The focus is on formulating rules best designed to achieve some lawful object of government. The process of legislation may entail codifying preexisting law, be it inalienable rights or general principles of law, but its distinguishing characteristic is that it designs positive enactments to best achieve legitimate government objectives. The second characteristic that distinguishes the legislative from the judicial process is that legislation is framed in general terms regulating all persons similarly situated.
>
> The process of adjudication, on the other hand, has a focus that is backward-looking in nature. Adjudication is designed to determine what happened to a relatively limited number of persons at some discrete time in the past. A court applies already existing law, be it acts of Congress, general principles of law, or the Constitution, to the facts of a case in order to determine whether a legal duty has been breached. If it has been, the court applies a remedy focused on restoring the victim, not achieving some future objective. Adjudication applies with particularity to a limited number of persons who are parties to a lawsuit.

---

[1] Dean Tuomala is a faculty member at Liberty University School of Law. He was the Law School's founding Associate Dean for Academic Affairs.

The exercise of the executive power, which like the exercise of the legislative power is forward-looking in nature, is designed to best achieve the legislative objects. The executive and legislative powers, as well as the power of appointment, are political or prudential in nature. . . .

Congress, in exercising the legislative power, makes judgments as to the best means of achieving constitutional objectives or ends. The President makes his best judgment in allocating resources and applying force to achieve those ends. . . . The judicial power does not entail the exercise of will (courts do not make law; the law already exists), and it does not entail the use of force (courts do not execute their own judgments; they depend upon the executive branch). Courts exercise only judgment—not political judgment that is forward-looking, but judicial judgment that is backward-looking in nature.

Jeffrey C. Tuomala, Marbury v. Madison *and the Foundation of Law*, 4 LIBERTY U.L. REV. 297, 329-330 (2010).[2]

A little later in his article, Dean Tuomala makes clear that the difference between judicial power (and reasoning) and legislative power (and prudential reasoning) is found, not only in the DECLARATION OF INDEPENDENCE, but also in the Scriptures and the person of God Himself. He writes:

Just as the doctrines of judicial review and general principles of law are grounded in the jurisprudence of the Declaration of Independence, so also is the doctrine distinguishing between the judicial and political powers. Civil officers exercise those powers in a manner that is reflective and imitative of the manner in which God governs the affairs of men and nations—as "Supreme Judge of the World" and as "Divine Providence." The exercise of judicial power as an application of established law to past conduct is demonstrated through the operation of the office of Supreme Judge of the World. In fact, the Declaration comprises the essential elements of a legal complaint—a statement of the judge's jurisdiction to hear the case ("Supreme Judge" with universal jurisdiction), a cause of action ("long train of abuses" that violated "unalienable rights"), and a remedy (independence/separation from England).

---

[2] I would highly recommend that you read this important article by Dean Tuomala in its entirety. It is absolutely essential to understanding law and the American system.

God also directs and governs, by His will and His law, that which He has created. The reference to God as "Divine Providence" describes Him in that office as the One who sees the end from the beginning and governs all things toward their appointed ends. The signers of the Declaration of Independence, convinced of the rightness of their cause and bound to one another by oath, moved forward with a firm reliance on God's protection. The nature of political powers as forward-looking and directed to enumerated ends is demonstrated through the operation of the office of Divine Providence.

Tuomala, *supra*, at 331-333 (citing, among other authorities, *Revelation* 20:11-13; *Romans* 3:25-26 and 8:1-4; *Isaiah* 53:5 and 2:1-6; *Ephesians* 1:11; *Colossians* 1:17; and *1 Peter* 1:18-19.)

In *Bushey*, did the district court engage in judicial or prudential reasoning? Justice Friendly rejects the district court's approach. What approach does he use, judicial or prudential?

_____

_____

_____

_____

_____

2. The Right Kind of Reasoning Without a Foundation. The district court in the *Bushey* case engaged in a form of jurisprudential reasoning that we would now classify as economic analysis of law, often referred to as law and economics. Law and economics is the dominant jurisprudential thought system in our country today, and it generally sees no problem with judges engaging in prudential as well as judicial reasoning.

Judge Friendly, to his credit, refuses to engage in this type of reasoning. He has a better understanding of the proper role of the judiciary than many judges would today. He realizes that, instead of engaging in prudential reasoning, he needs to figure out what the rule of law is in the case so that he can then apply that rule of law to the particular facts at hand, i.e., judicial reasoning. In doing so, he looks not to policy arguments (which are prudential in nature) but to the "deeply rooted sentiment that a business enterprise cannot justly disclaim responsibility for accidents which may fairly be said to be characteristic of its activities."

While this may sound good, and indeed Judge Friendly did reject prudential reasoning and attempt to engage in judicial reasoning, his views on law as a whole left him with no where to turn in a case where the applicable law seemed inadequate. (Judge Friendly actually developed a foreseeability standard for answering these types of questions, which has not been widely followed.) In other words, his view of law is missing its foundation.

While Judge Friendly's jurisprudence is lacking in a foundation, the historic Western legal tradition, of which the American system is very much a part, does not suffer from such an infirmity. Again, Dean Tuomala's article is most enlightening:

> Because Jesus Christ is Creator, *John* 1:1-5, and Supreme Ruler, *Hebrews* 2:6-8, He is also Supreme Lawgiver, superior to Moses who was the first lawgiver. *Hebrews* 3[and] *John* 1:17. Jesus made it clear that He did not change the law. *Matthew* 5:17-20; 22:34-40. But in Him the truth did appear in the flesh, *John* 1:14, and in His flesh He bore the curse of the law. *Galatians* 3:13. *The origin of Western rule-of-law jurisprudence is grounded in the truth that there is a transcendent lawgiver. The general principles of law derive from the law of nature, whose author is Jesus Christ.*

Tuomala, *supra*, at 314 n.89 (emphasis added). Accordingly, to borrow a phrase from the DECLARATION OF INDEPENDENCE, the foundation for law in the Western legal tradition is to be found in the "law of nature and nature's God."

Further, Dean Tuomala states that:

> God's law not only provides the right to establish a framework of government, but it also identifies rights—life, liberty, and the pursuit of happiness—that the framework is designed to secure. God's law also provides other general principles of law that all courts possessing judicial power are to apply in deciding cases.

Tuomala, *supra*, at 314-315. Among these general principles of law are general principles of commercial law. These general principles of commercial law could have been most helpful to Judge Friendly, much more helpful than "deeply rooted sentiment," which is likely little more than human consensus—a foundation that has been used to justify some of the worst atrocities the world has ever known. *See, e.g.,* Jeffrey S. Tuomala, *Nuremburg and the Crime of Abortion,* 42 U. Toledo L. Rev. 283 (discussing Nazi atrocities that were committed under the color of law that were later found to be war crimes and crimes against humanity during the Nuremburg trials).

Looking to the historic Western legal tradition, which is based upon and grounded in a Christian worldview, can you think of any general principles of commercial law that might apply to the *Bushey* case? If so, would they change the outcome of the case?

_____

_____

_____

_____

_____

3. A Split in the Law. While most courts have not followed Judge Friendly's "foreseeability approach," as previously noted, the law in this area is not completely settled. Two approaches have come to dominate the law, the "motivation test" and the "work-related test." The motivation test looks to whether the agent/employee was motivated by some purpose to serve the master. If no such purpose exists, then the principal/employer is not subjected to *respondeat superior* liability for the agent/employees intentional torts.

In the work-related test, on the other hand, the motivation of the agent/employee is immaterial. Rather, this test focuses on whether the intentional tort was committed within work-related time or space. Usually this means that the tort was either committed during working hours, on the premises of the principal/employer, or both.

How would the *Bushey* case have come out under each of these two tests? (Judge Friendly addressed and rejected the motivation test, but he did not deal with the work-related test specifically, although his own test may sound somewhat like it at times.) Which of these two tests do you think is most consistent with a Christian worldview? Why? Are you happy with one of these tests, or would you propose a completely different test in order to make this area of law consistent with the Christian worldview?

_____

_____

_____

_____

_____

Chapter 3
Partnership Fiduciary Duties and the Goodness of Competition

Meehan v. Shaughnessy
535 N.E.2d 1255 (Mass. 1989)

The plaintiffs, James F. Meehan (Meehan) and Leo V. Boyle (Boyle), were partners of the law firm, Parker, Coulter, Daley & White (Parker Coulter). After Meehan and Boyle terminated their relationship with Parker Coulter to start their own firm, they commenced this action both to recover amounts they claim the defendants, their former partners, owed them under the partnership agreement, and to obtain a declaration as to amounts they owed the defendants for work done at Parker Coulter on cases they removed to their new firm. The defendants (hereinafter collectively Parker Coulter) counterclaimed that Meehan and Boyle violated their fiduciary duties, breached the partnership agreement, and tortiously interfered with their advantageous business and contractual relationships. As grounds for these claims, Parker Coulter asserted that Meehan and Boyle engaged in improper conduct in withdrawing cases and clients from the firm, and in inducing employees to join the new firm of Meehan, Boyle & Cohen, P.C. (MBC). Parker Coulter also filed a third-party action with similar claims against MBC and against Cynthia J. Cohen Cohen), a former junior partner, and Steven H. Schafer (Schafer), a former associate, who, among others, left the firm to join MBC.

After a jury-waived trial, a Superior Court judge rejected all of Parker Coulter's claims for relief, and found that Meehan and Boyle were entitled to recover amounts owed to them under the partnership agreement. The judge also found, based on the partnership agreement and a quantum meruit theory, that Parker Coulter was entitled to recover from Meehan and Boyle for time billed and expenses incurred on the cases Meehan and Boyle removed to their own firm. Parker Coulter appealed from the judgment, and we granted direct appellate review.

Although we are in agreement with most of the judge's reasoning and conclusions which he reached after lengthy and painstaking proceedings, we nevertheless reverse the judgment entered below and remand for further findings and a hearing, consistent in all respects with this opinion. This result follows from our conclusion, *infra,* that the judge erred in deciding that Meehan and Boyle acted properly in acquiring consent to remove cases to MBC.[1]

We summarize the facts as found by the judge. Aside from certain conclusions which the judge reached, and which we address in more detail below, the parties agree that these findings were warranted by the evidence. Parker, Coulter, Daley & White is a large partnership which specializes in litigation on behalf of both defendants and plaintiffs. Meehan joined the firm in 1959, and became a partner in 1963; his practice focuses primarily on complex tort litigation, such as product liability and aviation defense work. Boyle joined Parker Coulter in 1971, and became a partner in 1980; he has concentrated on plaintiffs' work. Both have developed outstanding reputations as trial lawyers in the Commonwealth. Meehan and Boyle each were active in the management of Parker Coulter. They each served, for example, on the partnership's executive committee and, as members of this committee, were responsible for considering and making policy recommendations to the general partnership. Boyle was also in charge of the "plaintiffs department" within the firm, which managed approximately 350 cases. At the time of their leaving, Meehan's interest in the partnership was 6% and Boyle's interest was 4.8%.

Meehan and Boyle had become dissatisfied at Parker Coulter. On June 27, 1984, after unsuccessfully opposing the adoption of a firm-wide pension plan, the two first discussed the possibility of leaving Parker Coulter. Another partner met with them to discuss leaving but told them their proposed firm would not be suitable for his type of practice. On July 1, Meehan and Boyle decided to leave Parker Coulter and form their own partnership.

Having decided to establish a new firm, Meehan and Boyle then focused on whom they would invite to join them. The two spoke with

---

[1] We repeatedly, later in this opinion, refer to "preemptive conduct" of Meehan and Boyle, as well as their "breach of duty." Undoubtedly these are accurate descriptions, but we do not wish to leave the impression that the MBC attorneys were unfair in the totality of their conduct in departing from the firm. For instance, we recount early in this opinion that Meehan and Boyle left undisturbed with their partners, and made no attempt to claim, a very large amount of business which Meehan had attracted to Parker Coulter. [This footnote has been renumbered from the original, and so throughout the case.]

Cohen, a junior partner and the de facto head of Parker Coulter's appellate department, about joining the new firm as a partner. They arranged to meet with her on July 5, and told her to keep their conversations confidential. The day before the July 5 meeting, Boyle prepared two lists of what he considered to be his cases. The lists contained approximately eighty to 100 cases, and for each case indicated the status, fee arrangement, estimated settlement value, and potential fee to MBC. Boyle gave these lists to Cohen for her to examine in preparation for the July 5 meeting.

At the July 5 meeting, Meehan and Boyle outlined to Cohen their plans for the new firm, including their intent to offer positions to Schafer, Peter Black (Black), and Warren Fitzgerald (Fitzgerald), who were associates at Parker Coulter. Boyle stated that he hoped the clients he had been representing would go with him to the new firm; Meehan said he would take the aviation work he had at Parker Coulter with him. Both stated that they felt others at Parker Coulter were getting paid as much as or more than they were, but were not working as hard. Cohen decided to consider the offer from Meehan and Boyle, and agreed to keep the plans confidential until formal notice of the separation was given to the partnership. Although the partnership agreement required a notice period of three months, the three decided to give only thirty days' notice. They chose to give shorter notice to avoid what they believed would be an uncomfortable situation at the firm, and possible retaliatory measures by the partnership. Meehan and Boyle had agreed that they would leave Parker Coulter on December 31, 1984, the end of Parker Coulter's fiscal year.

During the first week of August, Cohen accepted the offer to join the new firm as a partner. Her primary reason for leaving Parker Coulter to join MBC was that she enjoyed working with Meehan and Boyle.

In July, 1984, Boyle offered a position at MBC to Schafer, who worked closely with Boyle in the plaintiffs department. Boyle told Schafer to organize his cases, and "to keep an eye towards cases to be resolved in 1985 and to handle these cases for resolution in 1985 rather than 1984." He also told Schafer to make a list of cases he could take with him to MBC, and to keep all their conversations confidential.

Late in the summer of 1984, Meehan asked Black and Fitzgerald to become associates at MBC. Fitzgerald had worked with Meehan in the past on general defense work, and Black worked with Meehan, particularly in the aviation area. Meehan was instrumental in attracting Black, who had previously been employed by U.S. Aviation Underwriters (USAU), to Parker Coulter. Although Black had already considered leaving Parker Coulter, he was concerned about whether USAU would follow him to a small firm like MBC, and wanted to discuss his leaving Parker Coulter with the vice president of USAU. In October, 1984, Black and Meehan met with the USAU vice president in New York. They later received assurances from him that he would be interested in sending USAU business to the proposed new firm. Black then accepted the offer to join MBC. Fitzgerald also accepted. Schafer, Black, and Fitzgerald were the only associates Meehan, Boyle, and Cohen approached concerning the new firm.

During July and the following months, Meehan, Boyle, and Cohen made arrangements for their new practice apart from seeking associates. They began to look for office space and retained an architect. In early fall, a lease was executed on behalf of MBC in the name of MBC Realty Trust. They also retained an attorney to advise them on the formation of the new firm.

Boyle was assigned the task of arranging financing. He prepared a personal financial statement and obtained a bank loan in September, 1984. During that fall, two other loans were made on MBC's credit. Cohen, at the request of an accountant, had been trying to develop projections of MBC's expected revenue in order to obtain long-term financing. The accountant requested a list of cases with indications as to MBC's expected fees for this purpose. In November, Boyle updated and revised the list of cases he expected to take to MBC which he had compiled in July. The November list contained approximately 135 cases. The increase in Boyle's caseload from July to November resulted in part from the departure of a Parker Coulter attorney in early September, 1984. Boyle was in charge of reassigning the cases this attorney worked on. Although another attorney requested transfer of some of these cases, Boyle assigned none to that attorney, and assigned most of the cases to himself and Schafer. Meehan, Cohen, and Black also prepared lists of cases which they anticipated they would remove, and included the potential fee each case would generate for MBC.

Toward the end of November, Boyle prepared form letters to send to clients and referring attorneys as soon as Parker Coulter was notified of the separation. He also drafted a form for the clients to return to him at his home address authorizing him to remove cases to MBC. An outside agency typed these materials on Parker Coulter's letterhead. Schafer prepared similar letters and authorization forms.

While they were planning their departure, from July to approximately December, Meehan, Boyle, Cohen, Schafer, Black, and Fitzgerald all continued to work full schedules. They settled cases appropriately, made reasonable efforts to avoid continuances, tried cases, and worked on discovery. Each generally maintained his or her usual standard of performance.

Meehan and Boyle had originally intended to give notice to Parker Coulter on December 1, 1984. Rumors of their leaving, however, began to circulate before then. During the period from July to early fall, different

Parker Coulter partners approached Meehan individually on three separate occasions and asked him if the rumors about his leaving were true. On each occasion, Meehan denied that he was leaving. On November 30, 1984, a partner, Maurice F. Shaughnessy (Shaughnessy), approached Boyle and asked him whether Meehan and Boyle intended to leave the firm. Shaughnessy interpreted Boyle's evasive response as an affirmation of the rumors. Meehan and Boyle then decided to distribute their notice that afternoon, which stated, as their proposed date for leaving, December 31, 1984. A notice was left on the desk of each partner. When Meehan, Boyle, and Cohen gave their notice, the atmosphere at Parker Coulter became "tense, emotional and unpleasant, if not adversarial."

On December 3, the Parker Coulter partners appointed a separation committee and decided to communicate with "important sources of business" to tell them of the separation and of Parker Coulter's desire to continue representing them. Meehan and Boyle asked their partners for financial information about the firm, discussed cases and clients with them, and stated that they intended to communicate with clients and referring attorneys on the cases in which they were involved. Sometime during the week of December 3, the partners sent Boyle a list of cases and requested that he identify the cases he intended to take with him.

Boyle had begun to make telephone calls to referring attorneys on Saturday morning, December 1. He had spoken with three referring attorneys by that date and told them of his departure from Parker Coulter and his wish to continue handling their cases. On December 3, he mailed his previously typed letters and authorization forms, and by the end of the first two weeks of December he had spoken with a majority of referring attorneys, and had obtained authorizations from a majority of clients whose cases he planned to remove to MBC.

Although the partners previously were aware of Boyle's intention to communicate with clients, they did not become aware of the extent of his communications until December 12 or 13. Boyle did not provide his partners with the list they requested of cases he intended to remove until December 17. Throughout December, Meehan, Boyle, and Schafer continued to communicate with referring attorneys on cases they were currently handling to discuss authorizing their transfer to MBC. On December 19, 1984, one of the partners accepted on behalf of Parker Coulter the December 31 departure date and waived the three-month notice period provided for by the partnership agreement. Meehan, Boyle, and Cohen formalized their arrangement as a professional corporation on January 1, 1985.

MBC removed a number of cases from Parker Coulter. Of the roughly 350 contingent fee cases pending at Parker Coulter in 1984, Boyle,

Schafer, and Meehan removed approximately 142 to MBC. Meehan advised Parker Coulter that the 4,000 asbestos cases he had attracted to the firm would remain, and he did not seek to take certain other major clients. Black removed thirty-five cases; Fitzgerald removed ten; and Cohen removed three. A provision in the partnership agreement in effect at the separation provided that a voluntarily retiring partner, upon the payment of a "fair charge," could remove "any matter in which the partnership had been representing a client who came to the firm through the personal effort or connection of the retiring partner," subject to the right of the client to stay with the firm. Approximately thirty-nine of the 142 contingent fee cases removed to MBC came to Parker Coulter at least in part through the personal efforts or connections of Parker Coulter attorneys other than Meehan, Boyle, Cohen, Schafer, Black, or Fitzgerald. In all the cases removed to MBC, however, MBC attorneys had direct, existing relationships with the clients. In all the removed cases, MBC attorneys communicated with the referring attorney or with the client directly by telephone or letter. In each case, the client signed an authorization.

Schafer subsequently separated his practice from MBC's. He took with him a number of the cases which had been removed from Parker Coulter to MBC.

Based on these findings, the judge determined that the MBC attorneys did not manipulate cases, or handle them differently as a result of their decision to leave Parker Coulter. He also determined that Parker Coulter failed to prove that the clients whose cases were removed did not freely choose to have MBC represent them. Consequently, he concluded that Meehan and Boyle neither violated the partnership agreement nor breached the fiduciary duty they owed to their partners. In addition, the judge also found that Meehan and Boyle did not tortiously interfere with Parker Coulter's relations with clients or employees. He similarly rejected Parker Coulter's claims against Cohen and Schafer.

1.   *Statutory Considerations; the Partnership Agreement.*

Before we address Parker Coulter's claims of wrongdoing, we first review the statutory right a partner has to cease his or her association with a partnership, and the statutory right the partner has to assets of the partnership upon leaving. We then examine how the partners in this case have modified these statutory rights in their partnership agreement.

General Laws c. 108A (1986 ed.) governs the formation, conduct, and liquidation of partnerships. Under § 29,[2] a "change in the relation of

---

[2] [The court is here discussing the Uniform Partnership Act (1914) (usually referred to as the UPA) as enacted in Massachusetts at the time of the case. A majority of states have now enacted the UPA (1997), a significant revision of the UPA which is

the partners caused by any partner ceasing to be associated in the carrying on ... of the business" results in dissolution of the partnership. The statute enumerates specific changes which cause a dissolution. A partnership may be dissolved at any time, for example, by the express will of a partner. G.L. c. 108A, § 31(1)(*b*), (2).

Where a partnership agreement provides that the partnership is to continue indefinitely, and the partnership is therefore "at will," a partner has the right to dissolve the partnership, and the dissolution occurs "[w]ithout violation of the agreement between the partners." G.L. c. 108A, § 31(1). . . . In a dissolution which occurs "[w]ithout violation of the agreement," the statute expressly defers to the method of dividing the partnership's assets which the parties bargained for in their partnership agreement. G.L. c. 108A, § 38(1). In contrast, where the partnership agreement provides that the partnership is to continue for a definite term, a partner has merely the power to dissolve, and the dissolution occurs "[i]n contravention of the agreement between the partners." G.L. c. 108A, § 31(2). If the dissolution occurs in contravention of the agreement, the dissolving partner is subject to certain damages, and the statute does not expressly allow the partnership agreement to control the division of the partnership's assets. G.L. c. 108A, § 38(2). . . .

In addition to giving a partner the power to dissolve a partnership, and to specifying the effects of a premature dissolution, c. 108A also provides a method for dividing the assets of a dissolved partnership. In the absence of an agreement otherwise, upon dissolution a partner may liquidate the partnership's assets and obtain his or her share of the surplus. G.L. c. 108A, § 38(1). Because it may be impossible to liquidate certain partnership assets immediately, the statute provides that "[o]n dissolution [a] partnership is not terminated, but continues until the winding-up of partnership affairs is completed." G.L. c. 108A, § 30. Each partner has a fiduciary duty to wind up this unfinished partnership business solely for the benefit of the former partnership. G.L. c. 108A, §§ 18(*f*), 21, 35. . . . Once the windup is complete, the total value of the dissolved partnership's assets can be determined. Each partner then receives his or her share. G.L. c. 108A, §§ 18, 38(1).

The Parker Coulter partnership agreement provided for rights on a dissolution caused by the will of a partner which are different from those c. 108A provides. Because going concerns are typically destroyed in the dissolution process of liquidation and windup, . . . the agreement minimizes the impact of this process. The agreement provides for an allocation to the departing partner of a share of the firm's current net income, and a return of his or her capital contributions. In addition, the agreement also recognizes that a major asset of a law firm is the expected

---

usually referred to as the RUPA. Massachusetts, however, still uses the UPA as the basis for its partnership statute.]

fees it will receive from unfinished business currently being transacted. Instead of assigning a value to the departing partner's interest in this unfinished business, or waiting for the unfinished business to be "wound up" and liquidated, which is the method of division c. 108A provides, the agreement gives the partner the right to remove any case which came to the firm "through the personal effort or connection" of the partner, if the partner compensates the dissolved partnership "for the services to and expenditures for the client." Once the partner has removed a case, the agreement provides that the partner is entitled to retain all future fees in the case, with the exception of the "fair charge" owed to the dissolved firm.

Although the provision in the partnership agreement which divides the dissolved firm's unfinished business does not expressly apply to the removal of cases which did not come to Parker Coulter through the efforts of the departing partner, we believe that the parties intended this provision to apply to these cases also. We interpret this provision to cover these additional cases for two reasons. First, according to the Canons of Ethics and Disciplinary Rules Regulating the Practice of Law (S.J.C. Rule 3:07, Canon 2, as amended through 398 Mass. 1108 [1986]), a lawyer may not participate in an agreement which restricts the right of a lawyer to practice law after the termination of a relationship created by the agreement. One reason for this rule is to protect the public. . . . The strong public interest in allowing clients to retain counsel of their choice outweighs any professional benefits derived from a restrictive covenant. Thus, the Parker Coulter partners could not restrict a departing partner's right to remove any clients who freely choose to retain him or her as their legal counsel. Second, we believe the agreement's carefully drawn provisions governing dissolution and the division of assets indicate the partners' strong intent not to allow the provisions of c. 108A concerning liquidation and wind-up to govern any portion of the dissolved firm's unfinished business. Therefore, based on the partners' intent, and on the prohibition against restrictive covenants between attorneys, we interpret the agreement to provide that, upon the payment of a fair charge, any case may be removed regardless of whether the case came to the firm through the personal efforts of the departing partner. This privilege to remove, as is shown in our later discussion, is of course dependent upon the partner's compliance with fiduciary obligations.

Under the agreement, therefore, a partner who separates his or her practice from that of the firm receives (1) the right to his or her capital contribution, (2) the right to a share of the net income to which the dissolved partnership is currently entitled, and (3) the right to a portion of the firm's unfinished business, and in exchange gives up all other rights in the dissolved firm's remaining assets. As to (3) above, "unfinished business," the partner gives up all right to proceeds from any unfinished business of the dissolved firm which the new, surviving firm retains.

Under the agreement, the old firm's unfinished business is, in effect, "wound up" immediately; the departing partner takes certain of the unfinished business of the old, dissolved Parker Coulter on the payment of a "fair charge," and the new, surviving Parker Coulter takes the remainder of the old partnership's unfinished business. The two entities surviving after the dissolution possess "new business," unconnected with that of the old firm, and the former partners no longer have a continuing fiduciary obligation to windup for the benefit of each other the business they shared in their former partnership.

In sum, the statute gives a partner the power to dissolve a partnership at any time. Under the statute, the assets of the dissolved partnership are divided among the former partners through the process of liquidation and windup. The statute, however, allows partners to design their own methods of dividing assets and, provided the dissolution is not premature, expressly states that the partners' method controls. Here, the partners have fashioned a division method which immediately winds up unfinished business, allows for a quick separation of the surviving practices, and minimizes the disruptive impact of a dissolution.

2.   *Fiduciary Duties; Breach.*

We now consider Parker Coulter's claims of wrongdoing. Parker Coulter claims that the judge erred in finding that Meehan, Boyle, Cohen, and Schafer fulfilled their fiduciary duties to the former partnership. In particular, Parker Coulter argues that these attorneys breached their duties (1) by improperly handling cases for their own, and not the partnership's benefit, (2) by secretly competing with the partnership, and (3) by unfairly acquiring from clients and referring attorneys consent to withdraw cases to MBC. We do not agree with Parker Coulter's first two arguments but agree with the third. We first address the claims against Meehan and Boyle, and then turn to those against Cohen and Schafer.

It is well settled that partners owe each other a fiduciary duty of "the utmost good faith and loyalty." . . . As a fiduciary, a partner must consider his or her partners' welfare, and refrain from acting for purely private gain. . . . Partners thus "may not act out of avarice, expediency or self-interest in derogation of their duty of loyalty." . . . Meehan and Boyle owed their copartners at Parker Coulter a duty of the utmost good faith and loyalty, and were obliged to consider their copartners' welfare, and not merely their own.

Parker Coulter first argues that Meehan and Boyle violated their fiduciary duty by handling cases for their own benefit, and challenges the judge's finding that no manipulation occurred.[3] . . . The judge's

---

[3] The judge found, specifically, that: "MBC, Schafer, Black and Fitzgerald worked full schedules from July to November 30, 1984, and some beyond. There was no

determination was one of fact, and was based on the assessment of the credibility of individuals with personal knowledge of the facts about which they were testifying. . . .

Parker Coulter also claims that we should disregard the judge's finding of no manipulation because the finding is clearly contradicted by other subsidiary findings, namely that Boyle planned to, and told Schafer to, handle cases for resolution at MBC rather than at Parker Coulter; that Boyle reassigned a number of a departing attorney's cases to himself and Schafer; and that a number of cases which were ready to resolve at Parker Coulter were, in fact, not resolved there. We do not agree that there is a conflict. The judge's finding that Boyle spoke of engaging in improper conduct does not require the conclusion that this conduct actually took place. Similarly, his finding that the reassignment of cases did not establish manipulation is consistent with a determination that the reassignment was based on merit and workload. Furthermore, the judge's finding that the MBC attorneys worked full schedules provides a reason for the delayed resolution of certain cases other than the improper motivation which Parker Coulter urges. Finally, Parker Coulter points to no specific case which the MBC attorneys manipulated for their own benefit. There is thus no contradiction between the judge's findings. We have reviewed the record, and conclude that the judge was warranted in determining that Meehan and Boyle handled cases no differently as a result of their decision to leave Parker Coulter, and that they thus fulfilled their fiduciary duty in this respect.

Parker Coulter next argues that the judge's findings compel the conclusion that Meehan and Boyle breached their fiduciary duty not to compete with their partners by secretly setting up a new firm during their tenure at Parker Coulter. We disagree. We have stated that fiduciaries may plan to compete with the entity to which they owe allegiance, "provided that in the course of such arrangements they [do] not otherwise act in violation of their fiduciary duties." . . . Here, the judge found that Meehan and Boyle made certain logistical arrangements for the establishment of MBC. These arrangements included executing a lease for MBC's office, preparing lists of clients expected to leave Parker Coulter for MBC, and obtaining financing on the basis of these lists. We believe these logistical arrangements to establish a physical plant for the new firm were permissible . . . especially in light of the attorneys' obligation to represent adequately any clients who might continue to retain them on their departure from Parker Coulter. . . . There was no error in the

---

manipulation of the cases nor were the cases handled differently as a result of the decision by MBC to leave Parker Coulter. They tried cases, worked on discovery, settled cases and made reasonable efforts to avoid continuances, to try their cases when reached, and settle where appropriate and in general maintain the same level of industry and professionalism that they had always demonstrated."

judge's determination that this conduct did not violate the partners' fiduciary duty.[4]

Lastly, Parker Coulter argues that the judge's findings compel the conclusion that Meehan and Boyle breached their fiduciary duties by unfairly acquiring consent from clients to remove cases from Parker Coulter. We agree that Meehan and Boyle, through their preparation for obtaining clients' consent, their secrecy concerning which clients they intended to take, and the substance and method of their communications with clients, obtained an unfair advantage over their former partners in breach of their fiduciary duties.

A partner has an obligation to "render on demand true and full information of all things affecting the partnership to any partner." G.L. c. 108A, § 20. . . . On three separate occasions Meehan affirmatively denied to his partners, on their demand, that he had any plans for leaving the partnership. During this period of secrecy, Meehan and Boyle made preparations for obtaining removal authorizations from clients. Meehan traveled to New York to meet with a representative of USAU and interest him in the new firm. Boyle prepared form letters on Parker Coulter's letterhead for authorizations from prospective MBC clients. Thus, they were "ready to move" the instant they gave notice to their partners. . . .

On giving their notice, Meehan and Boyle continued to use their position of trust and confidence to the disadvantage of Parker Coulter. The two immediately began communicating with clients and referring attorneys. Boyle delayed providing his partners with a list of clients he intended to solicit until mid-December, by which time he had obtained authorization from a majority of the clients.

Finally, the content of the letter sent to the clients was unfairly prejudicial to Parker Coulter. The ABA Committee on Ethics and Professional Responsibility, in Informal Opinion 1457 (April 29, 1980), set forth ethical standards for attorneys announcing a change in professional association.[5] Because this standard is intended primarily to protect

---

[4] Parker Coulter also argues that Meehan and Boyle impermissibly competed with the firm by inducing its employees to join MBC. Because Parker Coulter identifies no specific loss resulting from this claimed breach . . ., we need not address this issue.

[5] These standards provide the following guidelines for notice to clients:

> (a) the notice is mailed; (b) the notice is sent only to persons with whom the lawyer had an active lawyer-client relationship immediately before the change in the lawyer's professional association; (c) the notice is clearly related to open and pending matters for which the lawyer had direct professional responsibility to the client immediately before the change; (d) the notice is sent promptly after the change; (e) the notice does not urge the client to sever a relationship with the lawyer's former firm and does not recommend the lawyer's employment (although it indicates the lawyer's willingness to continue his responsibility for the matters); (f) the notice makes it clear that the client has the right to

clients, proof by Parker Coulter of a technical violation of this standard does not aid them in their claims. . . . We will, however, look to this standard for general guidelines as to what partners are entitled to expect from each other concerning their joint clients on the division of their practice. The ethical standard provides that any notice explain to a client that he or she has the right to decide who will continue the representation. Here, the judge found that the notice did not "clearly present to the clients the choice they had between remaining at Parker Coulter or moving to the new firm." By sending a one-side announcement, on Parker Coulter letterhead, so soon after notice of their departure, Meehan and Boyle excluded their partners from effectively presenting their services as an alternative to those of Meehan and Boyle.

Meehan and Boyle could have foreseen that the news of their departure would cause a certain amount of confusion and disruption among their partners. The speed and preemptive character of their campaign to acquire clients' consent took advantage of their partners' confusion. By engaging in these preemptive tactics, Meehan and Boyle violated the duty of utmost good faith and loyalty which they owed their partners. Therefore, we conclude that the judge erred in deciding that Meehan and Boyle acted properly in acquiring consent to remove cases to MBC.

We next consider Parker Coulter's claims against Cohen and Schafer. We have determined that "[e]mployees occupying a position of trust and confidence owe a duty of loyalty to their employer and must protect the interests of their employer." . . . Cohen was a junior partner, and acting head of Parker Coulter's appellate department. Schafer was an associate responsible for a substantial case load. Both had access to clients and information concerning clients and therefore occupied positions of trust and confidence. We conclude that their participation in the preemptive tactics of Meehan and Boyle violated the duty they owed the partnership.

. . . [In a lengthy section that is omitted, the court discussed the proper remedies and consequences for the breach of fiduciary duties.]

SO ORDERED.

---

decide who will complete or continue the matters; and (g) the notice is brief, dignified, and not disparaging of the lawyer's former firm.

See also ABA Committee on Ethics and Professional Responsibility Informal Opinion 1466 (Feb. 12, 1981) (extending Informal Opinion 1457 to departing associates as well as partners).

NOTES AND QUESTIONS

1. When Two General Principles Conflict.   We   have already seen that an important part of the Western legal tradition involves reasoning from generals or universals to particulars.   These universal principles are found in the "laws of nature and nature's God," as stated in the DECLARATION OF INDEPENDENCE and discussed in Dean Tuomala's excellent article on *Marbury v. Madison*.[6] In addition, these general principles form a law above the law from which we can reason and to which we are all accountable. These universal principles of law do not just relate to human rights, but also include general principles of commercial and business law.[7] In the Western legal tradition, we have historically looked to the Bible as a preeminent source for understanding and knowing these general universal principles.

The case of *Meehan v. Shaughnessy* does not cite to the Bible, but it certainly deals with concepts from the Bible and the general principles of commercial law found in the "laws of nature and nature's God." One such general principle is that "it is required in stewards, that a man be found faithful." 1 *Corinthians* 4:2. This gives rise to fiduciary duties for agents, partners, directors, officers, and others.[8]

However, what should a court do when that general principle of "faithfulness" comes into conflict with another of the general principles of commercial law? In this case, that other general principle is that competition is a good thing.

But, does the Bible teach that competition is a good thing? Take a sporting event for an example, do we generally view it as a good thing when athletes compete in sporting events? The answer to both these questions is yes. In fact, in 1 *Corinthians* 9:24-27 and 2 *Timothy* 2:5, Paul uses competition in the context of sports as a positive example for how we should live the Christian life.

Further, it is true that the Bible contains a number of passages that condemn financial unfairness in the marketplace. For example, "A false balance is abomination to the LORD: But a just weight is his delight."[9] Certainly these passages serve as a warning regarding the

---

[6] Jeffrey C. Tuomala, Marbury v. Madison *and the Foundation of Law*, 4 LIBERTY U.L. REV. 297 (2010). This is one of the best and most important articles that I have ever read. I would strongly encourage you to read it if you have not done so already.

[7] *Id.* at 315-325 (for an excellent discussion of this in the context of *Marbury v. Madison* and *Swift v. Tyson*).

[8] Paul in this passage is actually referring to himself as a steward (which is very much like an agent) of the gospel and saying that he must be found faithful. Thus, he is recognizing an existing standard and using it approvingly. Scripture's approval should be sufficient to establish this principle as within the laws of nature and nature's God.

[9] *Proverbs* 11:1. For a list of other passages addressing financial unfairness, *see* Rodney   D.   Chrisman,   *Bible   Passages   Addressing   Financial   Unfairness,*

dangers that exist in a market. Humans are fallen, and fallen humans will do fallen things. We generally don't mean it as a compliment to the human race when we say, "that's just human nature."

But, in the warning, let us not miss the fact that a competitive marketplace is assumed in these biblical prohibitions. To state it differently, the Bible assumes that there is and arguably therefore should be a competitive (capitalistic we might say) market in place. It assumes that there will be several people competing to sell, for example, the best wool at the best price, and that this is a good thing that does not need condemnation. It condemns lying and cheating in the market, not the competitive market itself. Any good thing can be perverted to sin, but that does not make the thing itself evil.[10]

Thus, as noted earlier, the *Meehan* court is actually dealing with these two principles: (1) competition is a good thing and (2) partners (like stewards) must be found faithful, which involves not competing with the partnership. In order to determine whether Meehan, Boyle, and the others violated their duties to Parker Coulter, the court must determine how to properly apply these two general principles in a factual situation where they are in conflict with one another.

That said, how did the court resolve the conflict between these two principles? Do you agree with the resolution? Does it depend upon whether you imagine yourself in the position of a person wanting to start a new business or one whose employee or partner is leaving to start a new business? How would you have ruled if you had been on the court?

_____

_____

_____

_____

_____

2. A Different Resolution in New York? Not all courts would resolve the conflict between these two general principles the way the Massachusetts Supreme Court did. For example, in *Gibbs v. Breed,*

RODNEYCHRISMAN.COM   (December   7,   2011), http://www.rodneychrisman.com/2011/12/07/bible-passages-addressing-financial-unfairness/.

[10] For more on the goodness of competition and other aspects of business enterprise, *see* WAYNE GRUDEM, BUSINESS FOR THE GLORY OF GOD: THE BIBLE'S TEACHING ON THE MORAL GOODNESS OF BUSINESS (2003) (chapter 8 of this excellent little book deals with competition). Further, for a discussion of the goodness of money, which addresses many of the same issues, *see* Rodney D. Chrisman, *Is Money Evil?*, RODNEYCHRISMAN.COM, http://www.rodneychrisman.com/articles/is-money-evil/ (last visited December 7, 2011, 11:10 A.M.).

Abbott & Morgan, 710 N.Y.S.2d 578 (Sup. Ct. 2000), the court came out somewhat differently in a similar case involving partners leaving a law firm. Read the following excerpt, and compare the holding and reasoning of the court in New York with the Massachusetts Supreme Court's holding and reasoning in *Meehan v. Shaughnessy*.

> Defendants did not establish that Gibbs breached any duty to BAM [Bredd, Abbott, and Morgan, the law firm from which Gibbs and Sheehan withdrew] by discussing with Sheehan a joint move to another firm, or that Sheehan's decision was based upon anything other than his own personal interests. In addition, while in certain situations "[A] lawyer's removal or copying, without the firm's consent, of materials from a law firm that do not belong to the lawyer, that are the property of the law firm, and that are intended by the lawyer to be used in his new affiliation, could constitute dishonesty, which is professional misconduct under [Model] Rule 8.4(c)" (D.C. Bar Legal Ethics Comm. Op. 273 at 192), here, the partners took their desk copies of recent correspondence with the good faith belief that they were entitled to do so.
>
> Contrary to the finding of the trial court, and applying the principle that "[t]he distinction between motive and process is critical to a realistic application of fiduciary duties" . . ., we find no breach of duty in plaintiffs' taking their desk files. These were comprised of duplicates of material maintained in individual client files, the partnership agreement was silent as to these documents, and removal was apparently common practice for departing attorneys . . . .
>
> However, the record supports the court's finding that both partners committed a breach of their fiduciary duty to the BAM partners by supplying Chadbourne [the firm they ultimately joined], and presumably the other partnerships they considered joining, with the April 26, 1991 memorandum describing the members of BAM's T/E department, their salaries, and other confidential information such as billing rates and average billable hours, taken from personnel files. Moreover, a closer examination of the record does not support the dissent's conclusion that these partners did not engage in surreptitious recruiting. The partners may not have discussed with firm employees the possibility of moving with them prior to June 20, 1991, but they indicated to Chadbourne the employees they were interested in prior to this date, and Gibbs specifically

testified that he refrained from telling one of his partners, to whom he had a duty of loyalty, about his future plans to recruit specific associates and support staff from the partnership.

There is no evidence of improper client solicitation in this case, nor is it an issue on this appeal. Although the analogy could be useful in concluding that Gibbs did not breach his fiduciary duty to the partnership by working with Sheehan to find a new affiliation, the fiduciary restraints upon a partner with respect to client solicitation are not analogous to those applicable to employee recruitment. By contrast to the lawyer-client relationship, a partner does not have a fiduciary duty to the employees of a firm which would limit its duty of loyalty to the partnership. Thus, recruitment of firm employees has been viewed as distinct and "permissible on a more limited basis than ... solicitation of clients" . . .. Pre-withdrawal recruitment is generally allowed "only after the firm has been given notice of the lawyer's intention to withdraw" . . ..

However, here, Sheehan prepared a memo in April of 1991, well in advance of even deciding, much less informing his partners, of his intention to withdraw. There is ample support in the record for the trial court's finding that the preparation and sending of the April 26, 1991 memo, combined with the subsequent hiring of certain trusts and estates personnel, constituted an egregious breach of plaintiff's fiduciary duty to BAM. Moreover, it is not speculative to infer more widespread dissemination given Sheehan's trial testimony that the memo "was prepared in connection with talking to other firms", and that "he was sure the subject of staffing was discussed at firms other than Chadbourne". Sheehan's disclosure of confidential BAM data to even one firm was a direct breach of his duty of loyalty to his partners. Because the memo gave Chadbourne confidential BAM employment data as well as other information reflecting BAM's valuation of each employee, Chadbourne was made privy to information calculated to give it an unfair advantage in recruiting certain employees . . ..

While partners may not be restrained from inviting qualified personnel to change firms with them . . ., here Gibbs and Sheehan began their recruiting while still members of the firm and prior to serving notice of their intent to withdraw. They did so without informing their partners that they were disseminating confidential firm data to competitors. Their actions, while still members of the firm, were intended to and did place BAM in the position of not knowing which of their employees were targets and what steps would be appropriate for them to take in order to retain these critical employees. The dissent's analysis, that once the firm was notified of the partners' departure, there was no breach of fiduciary duty, is flawed. The breach occurred in April of 1991 and could not be cured by any after-the-fact notification by the fiduciary who committed the breach that he was withdrawing from the firm. Chadbourne still had the unfair advantage of the confidential information from the April 1991 memo, and still had the upper hand, which was manifested by its ability to tailor its offers and incentives to the BAM recruits.

Id. at 582-583. Based upon the quote above, would *Meehan v. Shaughnessy* have been decided differently if it had been in New York? If so, how and why? Do you agree with the New York court or the Massachusetts court? Should recruiting employees be treated differently than recruiting clients? Why or why not?

_____

_____

_____

_____

_____

_____

3. *What is the Proper Balance?* Balancing two important general principles like this can be exceedingly difficult, as the disagreement between the two cases demonstrates. In addition to the cases, consider the following general comments regarding leaving a company to form a new competing company:

> Competing with the corporation while employed by the company is also, as a general proposition, an elementary breach of an agent's duty of loyalty. After all, competing with one's employer seems the very definition of disloyalty. . . .
> While the basic rule is that employees cannot compete with their employer, it is not only allowable, but socially desirable, for former employees to compete with their former employer. . . .

There is an inherent tension between the rule that current employees cannot compete with their employer, and the rule that former employees can compete with their former employer. Typically, employees do not quit their job one day, wake up the next day, and then decide to go into competition with their former employer. Rather, the decision to go into competition with one's employer commonly occurs before one quits. Moreover, part of the process of making this decision often involves taking various steps to explore the viability of starting a competing venture. After all, it is highly embarrassing, not to mention economically disadvantageous, to find out after one quits that the competing venture is not feasible. Overlapping with steps to explore the viability of a competing enterprise, are steps to set up the competing business. In many instances, these constitute the same activities. For example, negotiating a lease for the new venture may serve both to give one an idea as to the venture's viability and to lay the groundwork to start the venture. Even if an activity is not necessary in order to decide to start the competing venture, the employee typically wants to do as much preparation as possible before quitting (after which, the employee might no longer receive a steady paycheck for a while).

Numerous courts have faced the question as to how far employees can go to prepare a competing venture without crossing the line and engaging in impermissible competition before the employee quits. Incorporating the new business and lining up its finances and facilities seem okay. Soliciting the employer's customers is unacceptable. Borderline questions involve soliciting one's fellow employees to leave and join the new venture, and notifying customers of the employee's intentions without soliciting their business. A practical problem here is that discussions with customers and fellow employees are often the most important activity the employee needs to undertake in order to decide whether he or she should leave and go into a competing venture.

Courts also often condemn employees for concealing from, or misrepresenting to, their employers, the employees' intention to leave and set up a competing business. This seems to follow as a corollary to the disclosure obligations of agents to their principals . . .. Still, there is a bit of unreality to expecting employees to disclose intentions which will prompt the employer to fire them. Indeed, one suspects this is an area in which there may be a substantial discontinuity between legal expectations and customary practice.

FRANKLIN A. GEVURTZ, CORPORATION LAW § 4.2.9(b), at 384-86 (2000). Prof. Gevurtz is discussing the general employment setting. How is this different than the cases we read? Does it make a difference that they were partners leaving a partnership, or is it more important that they were lawyers?

Thinking about this issue from a Christian worldview, and considering everything we have read, what would you do in Meehan's position? Now, assume you are in Shaughnessy's position, does your answer change? If so, does this help you to determine what the appropriate legal rule should be? *See Matthew* 7:12.

_____

_____

_____

_____

_____

_____

CHAPTER 4
THE DOMINANCE OF THE LLC

During the previous chapters, we have often considered what might seem at first blush to be highly theoretical or conceptual issues related to the Christian worldview of law.[1]   While this chapter also contains questions of theory and concept, it is primarily concerned with a very practical question: "which form of business organization is best for a client in a given situation and how should that entity be taxed?"

At first blush, this very practical question may seem to have very little to do with the Christian worldview. That conclusion, however, would be in error. The Bible is a very practical book, and it is concerned with every facet of our lives. There is no part of the universe over which Jesus is not Lord. *See, e.g., Matthew* 28:18. Accordingly, there is no part of our lives with which He is not concerned.

Further, we as Christians should be good stewards of what God has given us, and we should be about the business of being fruitful and multiplying and taking dominion over the Earth. *See, e.g., Genesis* 1:28-31, 9:1 and 7. A primary means for accomplishing these goals is through business enterprises.

Consider this: the Pilgrims and Puritans who settled what is now Massachusetts did so via the business organization known as a Joint Stock Company. Business enterprises have developed cures for various diseases. They have built skyscrapers that tower over the landscape like mountains and dug vast tunnels under the sea beds. Businesses have been essential in accomplishing this amazing level of dominion over the earth and helping us to be fruitful and multiply and fill the earth just as God commanded.

---

[1] Hopefully, however, as you have studied and considered the materials you have come to the realization that these conceptual or theoretical issues make very real differences in cases and therefore the lives of individuals. To put it another way, ideas have consequences.

Therefore, choosing the right business organization form and tax regime for a new business is very much a God-honoring endeavor. The following excerpted article has information that should be very helpful to you as you learn how to make this important distinction.

Rodney D. Chrisman, LLCs Are the New King of the Hill
15 FORDHAM J. CORP. & FIN. L. 459 (2010)

Introduction

A revolution has occurred in the world of business organizations law. The limited liability company (LLC) is now undeniably the most popular form of new business entity in the United States. This is amazing, especially because for most of America's history the general partnership and the corporation dominated the business organizations' landscape. Rising from near obscurity in the 1990s, the LLC has now taken its place as the new "king-of-the-hill" among business entities, utterly dominating its closest rivals. As the research reported in this article indicates, the number of new LLCs formed in America in 2007 now outpaces the number of new corporations formed by a margin of nearly two to one. In several "bellwether" states, the numbers are even more impressive. For example, in Delaware and Colorado in 2007, over three new LLCs were formed for every one new corporation formed. Only four states had more new corporations formed than new LLCs in 2007; ten states and the District of Colubia had ratios of new LLCs to new corporations formed in excess of four to one; Connecticut came in with the highest, at a ratio of new LLCs to new corporations formed of 11.826 to 1.

The number of general partnerships formed each year cannot be tracked since no filing is required. In 2004, Professor Howard Friedman noted that general partnerships were now unlawyered transactions. He wrote:

> The LLC can replace the general partnership with a business that furnishes all of the advantages of the partnership, but also provides owners with limited liability. The general partnership has essentially disappeared as a "lawyered" business form. General partnerships that exist today are either holdovers from pre-LLC days or they are businesses entered into informally without legal advice that by default are subjected to the rules found in the Uniform Partnership Act. The once-elaborately drafted partnership agreement

> has gone the way of the buggy whip and slide rule. It has
> been replaced by the LLC operating agreement.

That is presumably even more accurate today. Thus, one can safely assume that most general partnerships are unlawyered transactions because nearly any imaginable advantage to the general partnership form can easily be achieved in the LLC form but with the added benefit of limited liability. Given the small cost of forming and operating an LLC, this additional benefit is almost always worth more than the additional costs. In fact, this author has suggested before in his classes that the act of a lawyer forming a general partnership in most states may well amount to malpractice. Accordingly, the number of general partnerships formed by lawyers each year is presumably very small and inconsequential. Assuming that the formation of the vast majority of general partnerships occurs in unlawyered transactions, LLCs dominate general partnerships as well in terms of the numbers formed for even the simplest of business operations.

Other business forms have fared no better against the LLC. While data for hybrid and newer business structures is more difficult to compile, the data in this Article relating to limited partnerships (LPs) demonstrate that the LLC's dominance of these entities is even more staggering. For example, the number of new LLCs formed in 2007 outpaced the number of new LPs formed in that same year by a margin of over 34 to 1. In seventeen states, the ratio of new LLCs formed in 2007 to new domestic LPs exceeds 100 to 1. In every jurisdiction at least six new domestic LLCs were formed in 2007 for every one new LP. Such a level of dominance should be enough to nearly relegate the LP to the dustbin of history. Further, there is no other alternative entity on the horizon that shows the promise or potential to unseat the LLC as the new king of the hill.

The only areas that have not been dominated by the LLC are those of publicly traded companies, companies that plan to become publicly traded companies, and non-profit entities. Many state statutes now permit LLCs to be organized for non-profit purposes, but presumably the requirements for tax-exempt status are such that nonprofit corporations will continue to be the entity of choice in this area. Further, regarding publicly traded companies or emerging publicly traded companies, most, including this author, thought that this would forever be the domain of the corporation. However, cracks in the dam have begun to emerge. Should the LLC succeed in becoming a viable competitor to the corporation in the publicly traded arena as well, then the oft-desired comprehensive business organization code will have been realized, albeit in a very different path than many of its supporters had hoped.

. . .

Perhaps due to the inattention given the LLC in law school, within academia, and even within the practicing bar, numerous misconceptions exist regarding some of its most basic issues. This Article addresses one of the most basic misconceptions—namely, that LLCs are always taxed as sole proprietorships or partnerships. While there are promising signs that this is changing, much of the literature simply assumes that LLCs will be taxed as sole proprietorships while hardly recognizing that other possibilities are available by election. As the research in this article shows, the majority of LLCs are currently taxed as sole proprietorships and partnerships, but the number of LLCs taxed as S-Corporations is growing at an astonishing rate. This appears to be an area where another practitioner-driven revolution is in the making. This is an area, therefore, that desperately needs attention because properly drafting forms to organize an LLC as an S-Corporation is a challenging matter and is largely unaddressed in the available literature and forms books.

. . .

I. LLCs are the New King of the Hill: The Number of New LLCs, Corporations, and LPs Formed in the United States Between 2004-2007

For much of the United States' history, there were only two available choices for those wanting to form a new business entity with two or more owners: the partnership and the corporation. The partnership was the default form of business and provided the benefit of pass-through taxation, but lacked the important feature of limited liability. The corporation, on the other hand, required a state filing and provided limited liability protection but at the expense of double taxation. Thus, prospective business owners faced a dilemma: receive the benefit of pass-through taxation and risk their personal assets in the business; or pay the penalty of double taxation but protect their personal assets. Neither option was ideal.

Thus, a quest for a more satisfying option began. An early attempt at solving the dilemma came from the states in the form of the limited partnership. LPs provide limited liability protection for the limited partners, but there must be at least one general partner with unlimited personal liability. Further, limited partners who become too involved in the business run the risk of forfeiting their status as limited partners and its commensurate limited liability protections. Therefore, while the LP was an improvement in certain instances, it did not truly solve the problem.

Congress also tried to provide an answer by enacting Subchapter S of the Internal Revenue Code. Under Subchapter S, a corporation could elect to be taxed as a Small Business Corporation ("S-Corporation").

Congress has changed the requirements over the years, generally loosening them, but there are significant restrictions on who can own shares in an S-Corporation and what form those shares may take. Therefore, the S-Corporation tax regime did not fully solve the problem either.

Then came the LLC. LLCs started out rather inauspiciously, and for many years did not appear to be destined for anything more than a specialized area of law for certain business owners in certain industries. The hope of the LLC is that it would provide the protections of limited liability for all of its owners while securing the blessings of pass-through taxation as well. This hope was not immediately realized because the taxation of LLCs was uncertain under the Kintner regulations. With the promulgation of the "check-the-box" regulations, however, the issue of how the IRS would treat an LLC for tax purposes was clearly settled, and the LLC began its rapid and steady assent to its current status as the most commonly formed new business entity in the United States.

The following tables clearly demonstrate this fact, conclusively showing that the LLC has been the first choice for most prospective new business owners in the United States beginning as early as 2004. . . . Before presenting the data, it should be noted that this Data builds upon the excellent work of Professor Friedman in *The Silent LLC Revolution*. The data presented, in many ways, picks up where the data in that article leaves off. There are, however, a few distinctions worth noting. As Professor Friedman noted, his data suffered from the fact that both domestic and foreign new LLCs were often lumped together, making it difficult to get a good handle on how many new LLCs were truly being formed across the country compared with new corporations. Except where indicated, beginning in 2004, domestic and foreign entities were separated, thereby alleviating the problem with Professor Friedman's data. Finally, this Article includes a comparison with both corporations and LPs, thus giving the fullest picture possible of the current state of formation of new business entities.

. . . [To view all of the charts and diagrams referenced herein, please see the full version of the article available at: http://www.rodneychrisman.com/articles/.]

II. Another Revolution Brewing?
How LLCs are Being Taxed for Federal Income Tax Purposes

When there were just two options for state-law business organizations, there were two symmetrical options for federal income taxation of those business organizations. Corporations were taxed under Subchapter C of the Internal Revenue Code as corporations, and partnerships were taxed under Subchapter K of the IRC as partnerships.

Limited partnerships were essentially a special form of partnership and as such were taxed much as general partnerships again under subchapter K. Similarly, the S-Corporation tax regime was a special way to tax a state-law corporation and, as such, did not especially strain the link between state-law business entity form and federal income tax regime. A corporation was still a state-law corporation, and it was still taxed as a corporation albeit a special type of corporate taxation under subchapter S.

Once again, then came the LLC. The LLC was neither a form of a corporation or a partnership. In fact, it bore characteristics of both and also many characteristics that are all its own. Therefore, there arose a very difficult question: what tax regime should be applied to such an entity? Should it be taxed as a partnership or as a corporation? The IRS frequently wanted to tax LLCs and other such hybrid entities as corporations, and business owners frequently hoped for their LLCs to be taxed as partnerships. Regardless of who won those early battles, when it became clear that the LLC would not automatically be lumped in with corporations or partnerships and taxed accordingly the connection between state-law business organization form and federal tax regime was effectively decoupled. Furthermore, since Congress has not enacted some new subchapter covering LLC taxation, the decoupling has been confirmed.

For a period of time, this decoupling led to significant uncertainties due to the four-part test of the Kintner Regulations. With the repeal of the Kintner Regulations, however, and the promulgation of the "check-the-box" regulations, the new decoupling accepted by the service was effectively embodied in federal income tax law. Thus, what was formerly automatic, i.e., corporations are taxed like corporations and partnerships are taxed like partnerships, in reality, even if not fully grasped or thought of this way at the time, became a two-part analysis. First, what state-law business entity form should be used? Second, which federal income tax regime will apply to this entity? This decoupling has led to much confusion in regard to the analysis of the common planning challenge: which business organization form should be used for a new enterprise?

As the following diagram indicates, for corporations there was really no significant change. A corporation is an "association" for tax purposes and as such may not elect, even under check-the-box, to be taxed as a partnership under subchapter K. Therefore, if the state law business form chosen is a corporation, then there are only two tax options: the default C-corporation taxation or elective S-Corporation taxation.

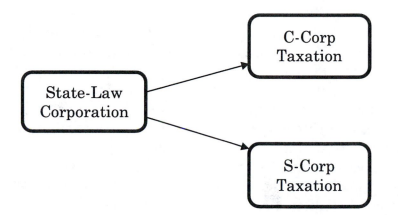

Most state-law corporations continue to elect to be taxed under the S-Corporation tax regime. This is primarily because the benefits of the C-Corporation tax regime are often far outweighed by the burdens of double-taxation. For example, in 2006, there were 3,909,707 S-Corporation returns filed as compared to only 2,009,500 C-corporation returns filed--a margin of nearly 2 to 1.

For partnerships and LLCs, however, the decoupling brought drastic changes. If the state-law business form chosen is a partnership or limited partnership, then there are three tax options: (1) the default partnership tax regime under subchapter K, (2) C-Corporation taxation, or (3) S-Corporation taxation. The following diagram illustrates the options available to a state-law GP or LP. Despite these options, it should be noted that the uses for general partnerships (and indeed limited partnerships as the data herein demonstrates) are very limited, and most GPs and LPs should probably be organized as LLCs.

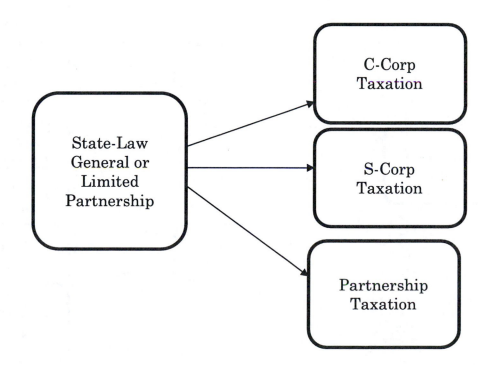

As stated above and noted elsewhere herein, one would assume that the vast majority of state-law partnerships and limited partnerships are taxed as partnerships. Further, as also noted elsewhere herein, a lawyer should mostly likely never form a general partnership. Any general partnerships are probably formed as the default organization and, therefore, not with the benefit of tax analysis and planning. Accordingly, it is likely that such entities would not make any tax elections. Additionally, LPs are becoming rarer and rarer, as demonstrated by the data herein, and the specialized circumstances in which they are still being used are likely well suited to partnership taxation. The IRS does not specifically track how many partnerships are being taxed as C-Corporations and S-Corporations, and the author of this Article did not request that data given the low-level of its significance for this article.

This decoupling's true effects are most dramatically displayed with regard to the LLC. If the state-law business entity form chosen is an LLC, then there are four options for taxation. First, the options available depend upon whether the LLC is a single-member LLC or a multi-member LLC. An SMLLC has three options: (1) default taxation as a disregarded entity (sole proprietorship on Schedule C to the Form 1040 for an individual), (2) C-corporation taxation, and (3) S-Corporation taxation. An MMLLC has three options as well: (1) default taxation as a partnership, (2) C-corporation taxation, and (3) S-Corporation taxation. The following diagram illustrates the options available to the LLC.

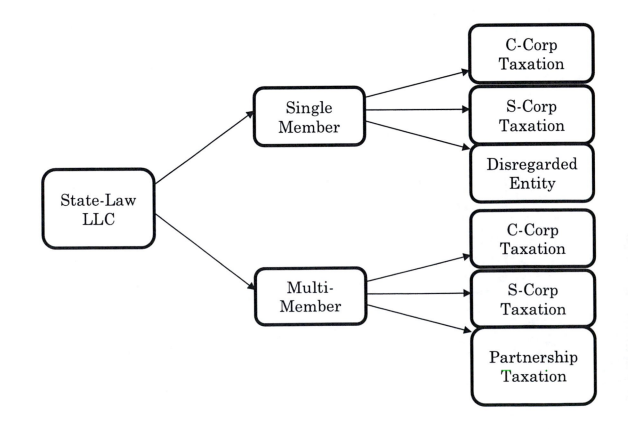

Following decoupling, most commentators and practitioners have assumed that little has changed with regard to federal income taxation of business entities other than the certainty brought by the "check-the-box" regulations. As the preceding notes, this is likely true for corporations, general partnerships, and LPs. Further, commentators also assumed that there would be little changes regarding LLCs as well. The assumption was that LLCs would likely follow suit and just be taxed as partnerships since that is what everyone wanted—partnership taxation with limited liability. The data set forth in the following, however, demonstrates that this assumption, while largely true, seems to be falling subject to somewhat of a revolutionary trend of its own—namely, as the effects and implications of decoupling become more widely known among tax practitioners it appears that more and more prospective business owners are being advised to use an LLC and elect to have it taxed as something other than a partnership. Generally, this something else is an S-Corporation.

. . . It appears . . . that practitioners are beginning to see benefits to the LLC state-law form beyond merely limited liability and partnership taxation that would make them want to use an LLC even when S-Corporation or perhaps C-Corporation taxation is preferable. For instance, the enormous flexibility and contractual nature of the LLC may provide advantages such as clearly negotiated and defined fiduciary duties and only the desired formalities. Further, in many states, the LLC may provide asset protection that goes beyond even that provided by the corporation.

Regardless of the reasons, the following tables clearly demonstrate that the trend is toward greater numbers of LLCs being taxed as something other than a partnership. . . .

NOTES AND QUESTIONS

1. The Dominance of the LLC. As the excerpted article points out, the LLC is the dominant business entity of choice for new business enterprises in America. This is because the LLC combines limited liability with pass-through taxation, among other benefits such as contractual flexibility and minimal formalities. The LLC will best meet the needs of most clients in most states, and therefore one would expect to see the number of new LLCs formed continue to increase overall and in relation to the number of new corporations formed. For an excellent discussion of the history of LLCs and their relative advantages over other business entities, *see* Howard M. Friedman, *The Silent LLC Revolution:*

The Social Cost of Academic Neglect, 38 CREIGHTON L. REV. 35, 39-56 (2004).

> If you were starting a new business in your state, which form of business organization would you choose? Visit http://www.rodneychrisman.com/articles/ and look at the charts provided in the article excerpted above. In your state, what form of business organization is most commonly used? The chances are very good that it is the LLC. Why are LLCs so popular?

_____

_____

_____

_____

_____

2. The Publicly Traded Exception. An important exception to the dominance of the LLC is that the vast majority of publicly traded businesses are organized as corporations. While it would conceivably be possible for LLCs to be used for publicly traded businesses, there are a number of things that currently make LLCs less attractive for these types of businesses. Therefore, one would not expect that corporations would disappear or cease to be an important form of business organization in America any time in the near future.

3. The Tax Question. As the above excerpt points out, there are three primary regimes under which a multi-member LLC may be taxed: partnership tax (under subchapter K of the Internal Revenue Code,) s-corporation tax (under subchapter S of the Internal Revenue Code,) and c-corporation tax (under subchapter C of the Internal Revenue Code.) C-corporation tax results in the dreaded double-taxation and provides only minimal countervailing benefits. Accordingly, c-corporation taxation is not appropriate for the vast majority of closely held businesses.

Therefore, most closely held businesses will need to choose between partnership and s-corporation tax. Determining which tax regime is best for a given business is a very fact specific inquiry, and a good working knowledge of the various advantages and disadvantages of each regime is necessary for effective tax planning. For an excellent article discussing the relative advantages and disadvantages of each form of taxation, *see* Walter D. Schwidetzky, *Integrating Subchapters K and S—Just Do It*, 62 TAX LAW. 749 (2009). For an excellent discussion of one of the primary benefits of s-corporation taxation for many closely held businesses, the minimization of employment taxes, *see* Timothy M. Todd, *Multiple-Entity Planning to Reduce Self-Employment Taxes: Recent Cases Demonstrate the*

Pitfalls and How to Avoid Them, 13 JOURNAL OF TAX PRACTICE & PROCEDURE 31 (April/May 2011).[2]

    Based upon the foregoing, if you were forming a new business entity, how would you elect to have it taxed? Is trying to minimize one's tax liability even a good thing to do? Is it biblical, or do we have a duty to maximize our tax liabilities? *See Matthew* 22:21.

_____

_____

_____

_____

_____

_____

---

[2] I am proud to say that Mr. Todd is a former student of mine, both at the Liberty University School of Law and School of Business.

CHAPTER 5
ARE LARGE CORPORATIONS DANGEROUS?

Louis K. Liggett, Co. v. Lee
288 U.S. 517 (1933)

BRANDIES, J. (dissenting in part) . . . The prevalence of the corporation in America has led men of this generation to act, at times, as if the privilege of doing business in corporate form were inherent in the citizen; and has led them to accept the evils attendant upon the free and unrestricted use of the corporate mechanism as if these evils were the inescapable price of civilized life, and, hence, to be borne with resignation. Throughout the greater part of our history a different view prevailed. Although the value of this instrumentality in commerce and industry was fully recognized, incorporation for business was commonly denied long after it had been freely granted for religious, educational, and charitable purposes. Fear of encroachment upon the liberties and opportunities of the individual. Fear of the subjection of labor to capital. Fear of monopoly. Fear that the absorption of capital by corporations, and their perpetual life, might bring evils similar to those which attended mortmain. There was a sense of some insidious menace inherent in large aggregations of capital, particularly when held by corporations. So at first the corporate privilege was granted sparingly; and only when the grant seemed necessary in order to procure for the community some specific benefit otherwise unattainable. The later enactment of general incorporation laws does not signify that the apprehension of corporate domination had been overcome. The desire for business expansion created an irresistible demand for more charters; and it was believed that under general laws embodying safeguards of universal application the scandals and favoritism incident to special incorporation could be avoided. The general laws, which long embodied severe restrictions upon size and upon the scope of corporate activity, were, in part, an expression of the desire for equality of opportunity.

[Justice Brandies describes the relaxation of requirements imposed upon business corporations. He notes that initially corporations were limited as to size, capital structure, powers, and purpose. He then details how these requirements were, over the years, relaxed.]

. . . Able, discerning scholars have pictured for us the economic and social results of thus removing all limitations upon the size and activities of business corporations and of vesting in their managers vast powers once exercised by stockholders—results not designed by the states and long unsuspected. They show that size alone gives to giant corporations a social significance not attached ordinarily to smaller units of private enterprise. Through size, corporations, once merely an efficient tool employed by individuals in the conduct of private business have become an institution—an institution which has brought such concentration of economic power that so-called private corporations are sometimes able to dominate the state. The typical business corporation of the last century, owned by a small group of individuals, managed by their owners, and limited in size by their personal wealth, is being supplanted by huge concerns in which the lives of tens or hundreds of thousands of employees and the property of tens or hundreds of thousands of investors are subjected, through the corporate mechanism, to the control of a few men. Ownership has been separated from control; and this separation has removed many of the checks which formerly operated to curb the misuse of wealth and power. And, as ownership of the shares is becoming continually more dispersed, the power which formerly accompanied ownership is becoming increasingly concentrated in the hands of a few. The changes thereby wrought in the lives of the workers, of the owners and of the general public, are so fundamental and far-reaching as to lead these scholars to compare the evolving 'corporate system' with the feudal system; and to lead other men of insight and experience to assert that this 'master institution of civilised life' is committing it to the rule of a plutocracy.

The data submitted in support of these conclusions indicate that in the United States the process of absorption has already advanced so far that perhaps two-thirds of our industrial wealth has passed from individual possession to the ownership of large corporations whose shares are dealt in on the stock exchange; that 200 nonbanking corporations, each with assets in excess of $90,000,000, control directly about one-fourth of all our national wealth, and that their influence extends far beyond the assets under their direct control; that these 200 corporations, while nominally controlled by about 2,000 directors, are actually dominated by a few hundred persons—the negation of industrial democracy. Other writers have shown that, coincident with the growth of these giant corporations, there has occurred a marked concentration of individual wealth; and that the resulting disparity in incomes is a major cause of the existing depression. Such is the Frankenstein monster which states have created by their corporation laws.

. . . Among these 200 corporations, each with assets in excess of $90,000,000, are five of the plaintiffs [who were chain stores complaining of a tax in Florida that taxed them more heavily than stores with less locations]. These five have, in the aggregate, $820,000,000 of assets; and they operate, in the several states, an aggregate of 19,718 stores. A single one of these giants operates nearly 16,000. Against these plaintiffs, and other owners of multiple stores, the individual retailers of Florida are engaged in a struggle to preserve their independence-perhaps a struggle for existence. The citizens of the state, considering themselves vitally interested in this seemingly unequal struggle, have undertaken to aid the individual retailers by subjecting the owners of multiple stores to the handicap of higher license fees. They may have done so merely in order to preserve competition. But their purpose may have been a broader and deeper one. They may have believed that the chain store, by furthering the concentration of wealth and of power and by promoting absentee ownership, is thwarting American ideals; that it is making impossible equality of opportunity; that it is converting independent tradesmen into clerks; and that it is sapping the resources, the vigor and the hope of the smaller cities and towns.

. . .

. . . The chain store is treated as a thing menacing the public welfare. The aim of the statute, at the lowest, is to preserve the competition of the independent stores with the chain stores; at the highest, its aim is to eliminate altogether the corporate chain stores from retail distribution. . . .

The plaintiffs discuss the broad question whether the power to tax may be used for the purpose of curbing, or of exterminating, the chain stores by whomsoever owned. It is settled that a state 'may carry out a policy' by 'adjusting its revenue laws and taxing system in such a way as to favor certain industries or forms of industry.' And, since the Fourteenth Amendment 'was not intended to compel the states to adopt an iron rule of equal taxation,' it may exempt from taxation kinds of business which it wishes to promote; and may burden more heavily kinds of business which it wishes to discourage. To do that has been the practice also of the federal government. It protects, by customs duties, our manufacturers and producers from the competition of foreigners. It protects, by the oleomargarine laws, our farmers and dairymen from the competition of other Americans. It eliminated, by a prohibitive tax, the issue of state bank notes in competition with those of national banks.

Such is the constitutional power of Congress and of the state Legislatures. The wisdom of its exercise is not the concern of this Court.

. . .

There is a widespread belief that the existing unemployment is the result, in large part, of the gross inequality in the distribution of wealth and income which giant corporations have fostered; that by the control which the few have exerted through giant corporations individual initiative and effort are being paralyzed, creative power impaired and human happiness lessened; that the true prosperity of our past came not from big business, but through the courage, the energy, and the resourcefulness of small men; that only by releasing from corporate control the faculties of the unknown many, only by reopening to them the opportunities for leadership, can confidence in our future be restored and the existing misery be overcome; and that only through participation by the many in the responsibilities and determinations of business can Americans secure the moral and intellectual development which is essential to the maintenance of liberty. If the citizens of Florida share that belief, I know of nothing in the Federal Constitution which precludes the state from endeavoring to give it effect and prevent domination in intrastate commerce by subjecting corporate chains to discriminatory license fees. To that extent, the citizens of each state are still masters of their destiny.

NOTES AND QUESTIONS

1. What Do You Think? The vast majority of wealth in America is still held by large, publicly traded corporations. In fact, it is likely true that the consolidation of wealth in the hands of large, multinational corporations is even more pronounced now than it was during the time of the Great Depression when the preceding opinion was penned by Justice Brandies. Do you agree with Justice Brandies? Is this a bad thing for freedom? For the economy? For small, closely held businesses? Or, is Justice Brandies just being an alarmist (which, given that this was written during the throes of the Great Depression, might be understandable)?

_____

_____

_____

_____

_____

2. The Privilege of the Corporate Form. Justice Brandies points out that the privilege of doing business in the corporate form is not inherent in citizenship. Another way to say this might be that the corporation (and indeed the limited liability company and other similar business forms) are created and authorized by the state and are not part of the laws of nature or nature's God. Since these entities are a creation of the civil government and therefore operating in the corporate form is a privilege, should the civil government be able to regulate them differently than it does a private individual? Should this include, as Justice Brandies suggests, the power to tax a corporation or class of corporations out of existence? These questions get at a more fundamental question: from the perspective of a Christian worldview, what is the proper role of the civil government in the economy? *See Romans* 13:1-7; 1 *Peter* 2:13-17; Roger Bern, *A Biblical Model for Analysis of Issues of Law and Public Policy: with Illustrative Applications to Contracts, Antitrust, Remedies and Public Policy Issues*, 6 REGENT U. L. REV. 103, 116-131 (1995).

_____

_____

_____

_____

_____

3. Separation of Ownership and Control. Justice Brandies also complains of the extreme separation of ownership from control in large business corporations. There are certainly real issues that stem from this separation. For example, a manager in a large corporation may be tempted to misuse the corporation and its assets for his own personal benefit as opposed to using and managing the corporation and its assets for the benefit of the shareholders, the owners. This is often called the "agency problem" in the academic literature of today, but it is not a new problem. *See Luke* 16:1-18. Even though this is an old problem, is Justice Brandies correct that large corporations with broadly dispersed ownership make this problem even worse? If so, what is a biblical answer?

_____

_____

_____

_____

_____

4. *Fiduciary Duties.* One answer that the law has developed over the years to the "agency problem" described by Justice Brandies is fiduciary duties. The law imposes upon managers (officers, directors, and others) a duty of care and loyalty with regard to their management of the corporation and its assets. In other words, it is required of a manager that he be found faithful. 1 *Corinthians* 4:2. We will consider the scope and reach of fiduciary duties further in the next chapter.

5. *Is Limited Liability the Problem?* One of the unique aspects of corporations is that they offer their shareholders limited liability, meaning that the shareholders liability is limited to their investment in the company. This undoubtedly contributes to the potential problems raised in this chapter. However, without limited liability, our financial system could not function. All of that said, is limited liability a biblical concept? Why or why not?

_____

_____

_____

_____

_____

_____

6. *Does the Danger Run Both Ways?* God entrusts us with property and expects us to use it for His glory. We have already noted the danger associated with the misuse of corporate assets by managers of the corporations. However, does this danger run both ways? In other words, is there a danger in giving the resources that God has entrusted to us to manage for His glory to others to manage for us? Is this shirking our responsibilities to God? Is this like gambling, only a legal version involving something like stocks? Or, is it a way for all of us to share in the profits of various enterprises across the country and around the world? *See Ecclesiastes* 11:1; *Matthew* 25:14-30; *Luke* 19:11-27.

_____

_____

_____

_____

_____

_____

7. *Are Large Corporations Dangerous?* Certainly large corporations have produced a number of products and technological breakthroughs for which we should be truly thankful. Consider, for instance, the computer on which this book was typed. Or, think of the many life-saving medical treatments that we have. Most of these things were developed and mass-produced by large corporations. Further, large corporations employ literally millions of people.

However, abuses in large corporations have caused much pain and suffering. In the Enron scandal, many people lost enormous amounts of money. Some lost their entire retirement savings. In addition, the current economic downturn, dubbed by some the Great Recession, was triggered, in part, by abuses in the investment and home mortgage industry. (Consider the question about the role of government in relation to this last sentence. Did the Federal Government's earlier interventions in the housing market play a role in the later financial disaster?)

After reading the opinion of Justice Brandies and considering the preceding questions and Scriptures, what do you think? Are large corporations dangerous? Should they be illegal? Closely regulated? Are they consistent with a Christian worldview? If not, what alternative system would you offer? If they are consistent with a Christian worldview, do you think there are abuses about which Christians should be concerned?

_____

_____

_____

_____

_____

_____

CHAPTER 6
THE BUSINESS JUDGMENT RULE AND THE PURPOSE OF CORPORATIONS

Shlensky v. Wrigley
237 N.E.2d 776 (Ill. App. 1968)

This is an appeal from a dismissal of plaintiff's amended complaint on motion of the defendants. The action was a stockholders' derivative suit against the directors for negligence and mismanagement. The corporation was also made a defendant. Plaintiff sought damages and an order that defendants cause the installation of lights in Wrigley Field and the scheduling of night baseball games.

Plaintiff is a minority stockholder of defendant corporation, Chicago National League Ball Club (Inc.), a Delaware corporation with its principal place of business in Chicago, Illinois. Defendant corporation owns and operates the major league professional baseball team known as the Chicago Cubs. The corporation also engages in the operation of Wrigley Field, the Cubs' home park, the concessionaire sales during Cubs' home games, television and radio broadcasts of Cubs' home games, the leasing of the field for football games and other events and receives its share, as visiting team, of admission moneys from games played in other National League stadia. The individual defendants are directors of the Cubs and have served for varying periods of years. Defendant Philip K. Wrigley is also president of the corporation and owner of approximately 80% of the stock therein.

Plaintiff alleges that since night baseball was first played in 1935 nineteen of the twenty major league teams have scheduled night games. In 1966, out of a total of 1620 games in the major leagues, 932 were played at night. Plaintiff alleges that every member of the major leagues, other than the Cubs, scheduled substantially all of its home games in 1966 at night, exclusive of opening days, Saturdays, Sundays, holidays and days prohibited by league rules. Allegedly this has been done for the specific purpose of maximizing attendance and thereby maximizing revenue and income.

The Cubs, in the years 1961-65, sustained operating losses from its direct baseball operations. Plaintiff attributes those losses to inadequate attendance at Cubs' home games. He concludes that if the directors continue to refuse to install lights at Wrigley Field and schedule night baseball games, the Cubs will continue to sustain comparable losses and its financial condition will continue to deteriorate.

Plaintiff alleges that, except for the year 1963, attendance at Cubs' home games has been substantially below that at their road games, many of which were played at night.

Plaintiff compares attendance at Cubs' games with that of the Chicago White Sox, an American League club, whose weekday games were generally played at night. The weekend attendance figures for the two teams was similar; however, the White Sox week-night games drew many more patrons than did the Cubs' weekday games.

Plaintiff alleges that the funds for the installation of lights can be readily obtained through financing and the cost of installation would be far more than offset and recaptured by increased revenues and incomes resulting from the increased attendance.

Plaintiff further alleges that defendant Wrigley has refused to install lights, not because of interest in the welfare of the corporation but because of his personal opinions "that baseball is a 'daytime sport' and that the installation of lights and night baseball games will have a deteriorating effect upon the surrounding neighborhood." It is alleged that he has admitted that he is not interested in whether the Cubs would benefit financially from such action because of his concern for the neighborhood, and that he would be willing for the team to play night games if a new stadium were built in Chicago.

Plaintiff alleges that the other defendant directors, with full knowledge of the foregoing matters, have acquiesced in the policy laid down by Wrigley and have permitted him to dominate the board of directors in matters involving the installation of lights and scheduling of night games, even though they knew he was not motivated by a good faith concern as to the best interests of defendant corporation, but solely by his personal views set forth above. It is charged that the directors are acting for a reason or reasons contrary and wholly unrelated to the business interests of the corporation; that such arbitrary and capricious acts constitute mismanagement and waste of corporate assets, and that the directors have been negligent in failing to exercise reasonable care and prudence in the management of the corporate affairs.

The question on appeal is whether plaintiff's amended complaint states a cause of action. It is plaintiff's position that fraud, illegality and conflict of interest are not the only bases for a stockholder's derivative action against the directors. Contrariwise, defendants argue that the courts will not step in and interfere with honest business judgment of the directors unless there is a showing of fraud, illegality or conflict of interest.

The cases in this area are numerous and each differs from the others on a factual basis. However, the courts have pronounced certain ground rules which appear in all cases and which are then applied to the given factual situation. The court in *Wheeler v. Pullman Iron and Steel Company*, 143 Ill. 197, 207, 32 N.E. 420, 423, said:

> It is, however, fundamental in the law of corporations, that the majority of its stockholders shall control the policy of the corporation, and regulate and govern the lawful exercise of its franchise and business. * * * Every one purchasing or subscribing for stock in a corporation impliedly agrees that he will be bound by the acts and proceedings done or sanctioned by a majority of the shareholders, or by the agents of the corporation duly chosen by such majority, within the scope of the powers conferred by the charter, and courts of equity will not undertake to control the policy or business methods of a corporation, although it may be seen that a wiser policy might be adopted and the business more successful if other methods were pursued. The majority of shares of its stock, or the agents by the holders thereof lawfully chosen, must be permitted to control the business of the corporation in their discretion, when not in violation of its charter or some public law, or corruptly and fraudulently subversive of the rights and interests of the corporation or of a shareholder.

The standards set in Delaware are also clearly stated in the cases. In *Davis v. Louisville Gas & Electric Co.*, 16 Del.Ch. 157, 142 A. 654, a minority shareholder sought to have the directors enjoined from amending the certificate of incorporation. The court said on page 659:

> We have then a conflict in view between the responsible managers of a corporation and an overwhelming majority of its stockholders on the one hand and a dissenting minority on the other—a conflict touching matters of business policy, such as has occasioned innumerable applications to courts to intervene and determine which of the two conflicting views should prevail. The response which courts make to such applications is that it is not their function to resolve for corporations questions of policy and business management. The directors are chosen to pass upon such questions and

their judgment *unless shown to be tainted with fraud* is accepted as final. The judgment of the directors of corporations enjoys the benefit of a presumption that it was formed in good faith and was designed to promote the best interests of the corporation they serve. (Emphasis supplied.)

Similarly, the court in *Toebelman v. Missour-Kansas Pipe Line Co.,* D.C., 41 F.Supp. 334, said at page 339:

The general legal principle involved is familiar. Citation of authorities is of limited value because the facts of each case differ so widely. Reference may be made to the statement of the rule in *Helfman v. American Light & Traction Company,* 121 N.J.Eq. 1, 187 A. 540, 550, in which the Court stated the law as follows: "In a purely business corporation * * * the authority of the directors in the conduct of the business of the corporation must be regarded as absolute when they act within the law, and the court is without authority to substitute its judgment for that of the directors."

Plaintiff argues that the allegations of his amended complaint are sufficient to set forth a cause of action under the principles set out in *Dodge v. Ford Motor Co.,* 204 Mich. 459, 170 N.W. 668. In that case plaintiff, owner of about 10% of the outstanding stock, brought suit against the directors seeking payment of additional dividends and the enjoining of further business expansion. In ruling on the request for dividends the court indicated that the motives of Ford in keeping so much money in the corporation for expansion and security were to benefit the public generally and spread the profits out by means of more jobs, etc. The court felt that these were not only far from related to the good of the stockholders, but amounted to a change in the ends of the corporation and that this was not a purpose contemplated or allowed by the corporate charter. The court relied on language found in *Hunter v. Roberts, Throp & Co.,* 83 Mich. 63, 47 N.W. 131, 134, wherein it was said:

Courts of equity will not interfere in the management of the directors unless it is clearly made to appear that they are guilty of fraud or misappropriation of the corporate funds, or refuse to declare a dividend when the corporation has a surplus of net profits which it can, without detriment to its business, divide among its stockholders, and when a refusal to do so would amount to such an abuse of discretion as would constitute a fraud or breach of that good faith which they are bound to exercise toward the stockholders.

From the authority relied upon in that case it is clear that the court felt that there must be fraud or a breach of that good faith which directors are bound to exercise toward the stockholders in order to justify the courts entering into the internal affairs of corporations. This is made clear when the court refused to interfere with the directors decision to expand the business. The following appears on page 684 of 170 N.W.:

> We are not, however, persuaded that we should interfere with the proposed expansion of the business of the Ford Motor Company. In view of the fact that the selling price of products may be increased at any time, the ultimate results of the larger business cannot be certainly estimated. *The judges are not business experts.* It is recognized that plans must often be made for a long future, for expected competition, for a continuing as well as an immediately profitable venture. * * * We are not satisfied that the alleged motives of the directors, in so far as they are reflected in the conduct of business, menace the interests of the shareholders. (Emphasis supplied)

Plaintiff in the instant case argues that the directors are acting for reasons unrelated to the financial interest and welfare of the Cubs. However, we are not satisfied that the motives assigned to Philip K. Wrigley, and through him to the other directors, are contrary to the best interests of the corporation and the stockholders. For example, it appears to us that the effect on the surrounding neighborhood might well be considered by a director who was considering the patrons who would or would not attend the games if the park were in a poor neighborhood. Furthermore, the long run interest of the corporation in its property value at Wrigley Field might demand all efforts to keep the neighborhood from deteriorating. By these thoughts we do not mean to say that we have decided that the decision of the directors was a correct one. That is beyond our jurisdiction and ability. We are merely saying that the decision is one properly before directors and the motives alleged in the amended complaint showed no fraud, illegality or conflict of interest in their making of that decision.

While all the courts do not insist that one or more of the three elements must be present for a stockholder's derivative action to lie, nevertheless we feel that unless the conduct of the defendants at least borders on one of the elements, the courts should not interfere. The trial court in the instant case acted properly in dismissing plaintiff's amended complaint.

We feel that plaintiff's amended complaint was also defective in failing to allege damage to the corporation. . . .

There is no allegation that the night games played by the other nineteen teams enhanced their financial position or that the profits, if any, of those teams were directly related to the number of night games scheduled. There is an allegation that the installation of lights and scheduling of night games in Wrigley Field would have resulted in large amounts of additional revenues and incomes from increased attendance and related sources of income. Further, the cost of installation of lights, funds for which are allegedly readily available by financing, would be more than offset and recaptured by increased revenues. However, no allegation is made that there will be a net benefit to the corporation from such action, considering all increased costs.

Plaintiff claims that the losses of defendant corporation are due to poor attendance at home games. However, it appears from the amended complaint, taken as a whole, that factors other than attendance affect the net earnings or losses. For example, in 1962, attendance at home and road games decreased appreciably as compared with 1961, and yet the loss from direct baseball operation and of the whole corporation was considerably less.

The record shows that plaintiff did not feel he could allege that the increased revenues would be sufficient to cure the corporate deficit. The only cost plaintiff was at all concerned with was that of installation of lights. No mention was made of operation and maintenance of the lights or other possible increases in operating costs of night games and we cannot speculate as to what other factors might influence the increase or decrease of profits if the Cubs were to play night home games.

. . .

Finally, we do not agree with plaintiff's contention that failure to follow the example of the other major league clubs in scheduling night games constituted negligence. Plaintiff made no allegation that these teams' night schedules were profitable or that the purpose for which night baseball had been undertaken was fulfilled. Furthermore, it cannot be said that directors, even those of corporations that are losing money, must follow the lead of the other corporations in the field. Directors are elected for their business capabilities and judgment and the courts cannot require them to forego their judgment because of the decisions of directors of other companies. Courts may not decide these questions in the absence of a clear showing of dereliction of duty on the part of the specific directors and mere failure to "follow the crowd" is not such a dereliction.

For the foregoing reasons the order of dismissal entered by the trial court is affirmed.

NOTES AND QUESTIONS

1. The Lights Come on at Wrigley Field (Eventually.) The lights did eventually come on at Wrigley Field, but it took another twenty years and an ownership change. The Chicago Tribune Company acquired the Cubs in 1981, which apparently removed P.K. Wrigley's objection to night games. However, it wasn't until 1988 (following pressure from Major League Baseball) that the first night game was played at Wrigley Field.[1] It is probably still unclear whether this improved the team's financial fortunes.

2. A Derivative Suit. This case involved a special type of lawsuit called a derivative suit. A derivative suit is most often a suit filed by a shareholder or group of shareholders on behalf of a corporation against the officers and/or directors of the corporation to enforce some right belonging to the corporation. Directors and officers control the corporation, and, due to obvious reasons, are reluctant to cause the corporation to sue themselves. Therefore, some mechanism is needed whereby shareholders can sue those in control of the corporation to enforce the rights of the corporation. To answer this need, courts of equity developed the derivative suit.

3. What Do You Think? If you were on the board of the Cubs, would you have voted to install lights? Should the court have forced the Cubs to install lights and play night baseball games? What do you think?

_____

_____

_____

_____

_____

4. The Business Judgment Rule. The business judgment rule as it is understood today is a deferential standard of review that is often described as a presumption. It is based upon the idea that courts should not be involved in the second-guessing of decisions made by corporate directors and officers absent bad faith, fraud, illegality, a conflict of interest, or failure to engage in a reasonable decision-making process.

---

[1] *See, e.g., Cubs Timeline,* CHICAGO.CUBS.MLB.COM, http://chicago.cubs.mlb.com/chc/history/timeline10.jsp (last visited November 22, 2011) and Phil Vettel, *The Cubs Get Lights at Wrigley Field,* THE CHICAGO TRIBUNE, August 8, 1988, *available at* http://www.chicagotribune.com/news/politics/chi-chicagodays-wrigleylights-story,0,866410.story. Ironically, the Cubs first attempt at a night game was rained out leading the Chicago Tribune to editorialize that "Someone up there seems to take day baseball seriously." *Id.*

Further, courts will assume that directors and officers make decisions in this fashion, i.e., free from these defects. The plaintiff must prove that one of these defects exist in order to overcome the presumption.

If the plaintiff is unable to overcome the presumption, most courts will only disturb the decision of the directors or officers if it amounts to a waste of corporate assets or lacks any rational business purpose. *See, e.g., In re The Walt Disney Co. Derivative Litigation*, 906 A.2d 27, 73-75 (Del. 2006). In other words, these courts apply a very deferential standard of review to these decisions. However, some courts will not review the merits of a decision at all absent one of the defects previously described. This is an even more deferential "abstention" standard of review.

This particular case is a little older and the business judgment rule was, at that point, a bit less clearly developed. However, the court does appear to be applying the business judgment rule. That said, which version of the business judgment rule does the court appear to apply here? The waste or rational business purpose standard or the more lenient abstention standard?

_____

_____

_____

_____

_____

_____

5. *The Fight Over the Lights.* The plaintiff alleges that attendance at Cubs' home games suffered (and therefore revenue suffered) because of the directors' refusal to install lights and play night baseball games. Are you convinced? Could there be other reasons? (Hint: look up the Cubs' records for the years in question.)

The court felt there could be legitimate business reasons for not installing lights and playing night baseball games. What were the ones the court suggested? Are you persuaded? Or, is the plaintiff correct that Wrigley was a baseball purest who opposed night games regardless of what it did to the team? What does this tell us about the business judgment rule?

_____

_____

_____

_____

_____

_____

> **6. The Christian Worldview and the Business Judgment Rule.**
In the previous chapter, we considered whether there are risks associated with the so-called "agency problem," i.e., the separation of ownership from control and the risks attendant thereto. In light of that, does this deferential standard of review make sense? Does it make sense from the perspective of a Christian worldview? Why or why not? What types of issues should we consider?

_____

_____

_____

_____

_____

> **a. Deference to the Market and Those Who Know it Best?** One justification often put forward for the business judgment rule is that courts are not business experts and should not substitute their judgment for the judgment of officers and directors (assuming, of course, no fraud, bad faith, or other malfeasance.) Are you convinced? For instance, courts commonly review (and substitute their judgment for?) doctors, and one presumes that most courts know even less about practicing medicine than they do about running businesses. Could it be that the courts are pointing to something else here?

It may well be that courts recognize that the market has a disciplining effect of its own on managers. Incompetent managers, not just fraudulent managers, have a way of getting fired. Directors and officers who incompetently run companies do not often remain directors and officers all that long. Shareholders vote them out, or another company takes over their company through some type of acquisitive transaction. In other words, competition is at work. Maybe the court is just recognizing that the market is a pretty efficient judge of management competency over time.

Further, courts are here recognizing the limits of all mankind by recognizing their own limitations. We are not God. We do not exhaustively know the future. (*See, e.g., Isaiah* 46:9-10. God clearly does know the future.) In fact, we have only a very limited understanding of the past and the present. What may initially look like a really bad idea may turn out to be a great one. Or, what appears to be a very reasonable strategy at the time it is entered into can turn out to be a disastrous miscalculation. Examples from the history of business abound.[2]

---

[2] For example, Fred Smith's idea for FedEx receiving a grade of C at Yale has become the stuff of business school legend. Compare *Fred Smith on the Birth of FedEx*, BUSINESSWEEK.COM   (September   20,   2004),

In fact, the best apparatus ever designed for figuring out what is a good and useful invention and what is not is probably the market. Good ideas tend to survive in the market (for example, the Apple iPad) and bad ideas don't (for example, the Apple Newton.)

Maybe a Christian understanding of this reasoning to support the business judgment rule should be something like, "Judges are not God. They do not know the future; none of us do. Therefore, they are not sure what ideas are good ones and what ideas are bad ones. God has given us the wonderful gift of the market to figure that out over time. Accordingly, they will not second guess decisions made by business managers absent some type of fraud or other malfeasance."

b. Encouraging Legitimate Risk-taking? Related to this previous point is that idea that some legitimate amount of risk-taking is a good thing. In order for many wonderful things to be done or invented, and in order that we might better take dominion over the earth, some amount of risk taking is required and is therefore a good thing. The business judgment rule operates to encourage legitimate risk-taking by protecting decisions that, while turning out badly, were made initially in good faith, after a reasonable decision-making process, and without conflicts or other wrong-doing. Thus, we might say that, in these instances, the business judgment rule looks only at the process but not the substance of the decisions of business managers.

On the issue of the business judgment rule encouraging an appropriate level of risk-taking by business managers, consider the following:

> While it is often stated that corporate directors and officers will be liable for negligence in carrying out their corporate duties, all seem agreed that such a statement is misleading. *See generally,* Lattin, *Corporations,* 272–75 (1971). Whereas an automobile driver who makes a mistake in judgment as to speed or distance injuring a pedestrian will likely be called upon to respond in damages, a corporate officer who makes a mistake in judgment as to economic conditions, consumer tastes or production line efficiency will rarely, if ever, be found liable for damages suffered by the

---

http://www.businessweek.com/magazine/content/04_38/b3900032_mz072.htm   with *Frederick W. Smith*, ACADEMY OF ACHIEVEMENT (January 9, 2008, 12:20 PM), http://www.achievement.org/autodoc/page/smi0bio-1.   Many other famous examples relating to technological innovations are often downright amusing. *See, e.g.,* L. Gordon Crovitz, *Technology Predictions are Mostly Bunk,* THE WALL STREET JOURNAL (December 27,   2009,   8:41   PM), http://online.wsj.com/article/SB10001424052748704039704574616401913653862.html. Apparently even business people have a hard time determining whether something is a good idea until after the fact.

corporation. *See generally,* Symposium, *Officers' and Directors' Responsibilities and Liabilities,* 27 BUS. LAWYER 1 (1971); Fever, *Personal Liabilities of Corporate Officers and Directors,* 28–42 (2d ed. 1974). Whatever the terminology, the fact is that liability is rarely imposed upon corporate directors or officers simply for bad judgment and this reluctance to impose liability for unsuccessful business decisions has been doctrinally labeled the business judgment rule. Although the rule has suffered under academic criticism, *see, e.g.,* Cary, *Standards of Conduct Under Common Law, Present Day Statutes and the Model Act,* 27 BUS. LAWYER 61 (1972), it is not without rational basis.

First, shareholders to a very real degree voluntarily undertake the risk of bad business judgment. Investors need not buy stock, for investment markets offer an array of opportunities less vulnerable to mistakes in judgment by corporate officers. Nor need investors buy stock in particular corporations. In the exercise of what is genuinely a free choice, the quality of a firm's management is often decisive and information is available from professional advisors. Since shareholders can and do select among investments partly on the basis of management, the business judgment rule merely recognizes a certain voluntariness in undertaking the risk of bad business decisions.

Second, courts recognize that after-the-fact litigation is a most imperfect device to evaluate corporate business decisions. The circumstances surrounding a corporate decision are not easily reconstructed in a courtroom years later, since business imperatives often call for quick decisions, inevitably based on less than perfect information. The entrepreneur's function is to encounter risks and to confront uncertainty, and a reasoned decision at the time made may seem a wild hunch viewed years later against a background of perfect knowledge.

Third, because potential profit often corresponds to the potential risk, it is very much in the interest of shareholders that the law not create incentives for overly cautious corporate decisions. Some opportunities offer great profits at the risk of very substantial losses, while the alternatives offer less risk of loss but also less potential profit. Shareholders can reduce the volatility of risk by diversifying their holdings. In the case of the diversified shareholder, the seemingly more risky alternatives may well be the best choice since great losses in some stocks will over time be

offset by even greater gains in others. Given mutual funds
and similar forms of diversified investment, courts need not
bend over backwards to give special protection to
shareholders who refuse to reduce the volatility of risk by not
diversifying. A rule which penalizes the choice of seemingly
riskier alternatives thus may not be in the interest of
shareholders generally.

Joy v. North, 692 F.2d 880, 885-886 (2d Cir. 1982). In support of the
preceding, the court offered the following example in a footnote:

Consider the choice between two investments in an example
adapted from Klein, *Business Organization and Finance* 147–
49 (1980):

INVESTMENT A			INVESTMENT B		
Estimated Probability of Outcome	Outcome Profit or Loss	Value	Estimated Probability of Outcome	Outcome Profit or Loss	Value
.4	+15	6.0	.4	+6	2.4
.4	+ 1	.4	.4	+2	.8
.2	-13	-2.6	.2	+1	.2
1.0		3.8	1.0		3.4

Although A is clearly "worth" more than B, it is riskier
because it is more volatile. Diversification lessens the
volatility by allowing investors to invest in 20 or 200 A's
which will tend to guarantee a total result near the value.
Shareholders are thus better off with the various firms
selecting A over B, although after the fact they will complain
in each case of the 2.6 loss. If the courts did not abide by the
business judgment rule, they might well penalize the choice
of A in each such case and thereby unknowingly injure
shareholders generally by creating incentives for
management always to choose B.

Id. at 886 n.6.

What do you think? Are you convinced by these justifications for
the business judgment rule? Are they consistent with a Christian
worldview? *See Genesis* 1:28-31; *Proverbs* 21:5, 27:23-24; *Ecclesiastes*
5:13-17, 11:1-2; *Matthew* 25:14-30; *Luke* 19:11-27.

_____

_____

_____

7. What is the Purpose of a Corporation Anyway? What is the overarching purpose of a corporation anyway? What should the officers and directors be endeavoring to do? What ultimate goal should they try and accomplish?

The interesting case of *Dodge v. Ford Motor Co.*, 170 N.W. 668 (Mich. 1919), discussed by the court in *Shlensky*, is a classic case on the question of the purpose of a business corporation. In that case, the Dodge brothers (yes, those Dodge brothers, as in Dodge Rams and Dodge Caravans) resigned as directors in the Ford Motor Co. and opened a competing car company. Undoubtedly due in part to a desire to avoid funding a competitor, Henry Ford stopped the policy that the Ford Motor Co. had pursued of paying large special dividends.[3] He also wanted to hold on to the cash to reinvest it in the massive River Rouge manufacturing facility that he planned to have Ford Motor Co. build. The Dodge brothers sued and asked the court to force Ford to pay dividends and to enjoin the building of the factory.

The court was inclined to follow the business judgment rule and therefore not interfere in the decisions of the Ford Motor Co. board. However, Henry Ford's own testimony made that course of action very difficult for the court. Ford was very concerned that he not be seen as a robber baron, and therefore his testimony gave the impression that he was not attempting to make money through Ford Motor Co. at all. Rather, he seemed to be asserting a position that the company should be run for the common good of the workers and automobile purchasers.

Given Mr. Ford's rhetoric and the rising tide of communism, the court seemed to feel that it simply could not defer to the board in this case. It did not enjoin the construction of the factory, which was built and remains the world's largest manufacturing facility. However, the court did order the Ford Motor Co. to pay the dividends. The court's reason for so holding was that the purpose of a corporation is to make money for the shareholders, or owners. Therefore, Mr. Ford was not free to run it as a semi-charity.

Dodge v. Ford is bad law on dividends. Virtually no court now would interfere with a board's determination with regard to dividends, as seen by the fact that many technology companies pay no dividends at all. However, while the principle has been somewhat eroded over the years, the case is still considered good authority for the proposition that the

---

[3] Confiscatory tax rates in effect at the time of World War I undoubtedly also impacted Ford's plans regarding dividends.

overarching purpose of business corporations is the maximization of shareholder wealth.

Is the maximization of shareholder wealth the proper purpose for corporations? Is it consistent with the Bible? If not, what should the purpose be? How does a biblical understanding of property rights affect your answers to these questions? *See Matthew* 20:1-16; Rodney D. Chrisman, *God Created Private Property and It is a Good Thing*, RODNEYCHRISMAN.COM (August 26, 2010), http://www.rodneychrisman.com/2010/08/26/god-created-private-property-and-it-is-a-good-thing/; and Rodney D. Chrisman, *Business is not Evil (Or Neutral)*, RODNEYCHRISMAN.COM (August 24, 2010), http://www.rodneychrisman.com/2010/08/24/business-is-not-evil-or-neutral/.

_____

_____

_____

_____

_____

CHAPTER 7
JUDGING DIRECTOR FAITHFULNESS IN TAKEOVER CASES

Paramount Communications, Inc. v. Time Incorporated
571 A.2d 1140 (Del. 1989)

Paramount Communications, Inc. ("Paramount") and two other groups of plaintiffs ("Shareholder Plaintiffs"), shareholders of Time Incorporated ("Time"), a Delaware corporation, separately filed suits in the Delaware Court of Chancery seeking a preliminary injunction to halt Time's tender offer for 51% of Warner Communication, Inc.'s ("Warner") outstanding shares at $70 cash per share. The court below consolidated the cases and, following the development of an extensive record, after discovery and an evidentiary hearing, denied plaintiffs' motion. In a 50–page unreported opinion and order entered July 14, 1989, the Chancellor refused to enjoin Time's consummation of its tender offer, concluding that the plaintiffs were unlikely to prevail on the merits.

On the same day, plaintiffs filed in this Court an interlocutory appeal, which we accepted on an expedited basis. Pending the appeal, a stay of execution of Time's tender offer was entered for ten days, or until July 24, 1989, at 5:00 p.m. Following briefing and oral argument, on July 24 we concluded that the decision below should be affirmed. We so held in a brief ruling from the bench and a separate Order entered on that date. The effect of our decision was to permit Time to proceed with its tender offer for Warner's outstanding shares. This is the written opinion articulating the reasons for our July 24 bench ruling.

The principal ground for reversal, asserted by all plaintiffs, is that Paramount's June 7, 1989 uninvited all-cash, all-shares, "fully negotiable" (though conditional) tender offer for Time triggered duties under *Unocal Corp. v. Mesa Petroleum Co.,* Del.Supr., 493 A.2d 946 (1985), and that Time's board of directors, in responding to Paramount's offer, breached those duties. As a consequence, plaintiffs argue that in our review of the Time board's decision of June 16, 1989 to enter into a revised merger agreement with Warner, Time is not entitled to the benefit and protection of the business judgment rule.

Shareholder Plaintiffs also assert a claim based on *Revlon v. MacAndrews & Forbes Holdings, Inc.,* Del.Supr., 506 A.2d 173 (1986). They argue that the original Time–Warner merger agreement of March 4, 1989 resulted in a change of control which effectively put Time up for sale, thereby triggering *Revlon* duties. Those plaintiffs argue that Time's board breached its *Revlon* duties by failing, in the face of the change of control, to maximize shareholder value in the immediate term.

Applying our standard of review, we affirm the Chancellor's ultimate finding and conclusion under *Unocal.* We find that Paramount's tender offer was reasonably perceived by Time's board to pose a threat to Time and that the Time board's "response" to that threat was, under the circumstances, reasonable and proportionate. Applying *Unocal,* we reject the argument that the only corporate threat posed by an all-shares, all-cash tender offer is the possibility of inadequate value.

We also find that Time's board did not by entering into its initial merger agreement with Warner come under a *Revlon* duty either to auction the company or to maximize short-term shareholder value, notwithstanding the unequal share exchange. Therefore, the Time board's original plan of merger with Warner was subject only to a business judgment rule analysis.

I

Time is a Delaware corporation with its principal offices in New York City. Time's traditional business is publication of magazines and books; however, Time also provides pay television programming through its Home Box Office, Inc. and Cinemax subsidiaries. In addition, Time owns and operates cable television franchises through its subsidiary, American Television and Communication Corporation. During the relevant time period, Time's board consisted of sixteen directors. Twelve of the directors were "outside," nonemployee directors. Four of the directors were also officers of the company. . . .

As early as 1983 and 1984, Time's executive board began considering expanding Time's operations into the entertainment industry. In 1987, Time established a special committee of executives to consider and propose corporate strategies for the 1990s. The consensus of the committee was that Time should move ahead in the area of ownership and creation of video programming. This expansion, as the Chancellor noted, was predicated upon two considerations: first, Time's desire to have greater control, in terms of quality and price, over the film products delivered by way of its cable network and franchises; and second, Time's concern over the increasing globalization of the world economy. Some of Time's outside directors, especially Luce and Temple, had opposed this move as a threat to the editorial integrity and journalistic focus of Time.[1] Despite this concern, the board recognized that a vertically integrated video enterprise to complement Time's existing HBO and cable networks would better enable it to compete on a global basis.

In late spring of 1987, a meeting took place between Steve Ross, CEO of Warner Brothers, and Nicholas [President and CEO] of Time. Ross and Nicholas discussed the possibility of a joint venture between the two companies through the creation of a jointly-owned cable company. Time would contribute its cable system and HBO. Warner would contribute its cable system and provide access to Warner Brothers Studio. The resulting venture would be a larger, more efficient cable network, able to produce and distribute its own movies on a worldwide basis. Ultimately the parties abandoned this plan, determining that it was impractical for several reasons, chief among them being tax considerations.

On August 11, 1987, Gerald M. Levin, Time's vice chairman and chief strategist, wrote J. Richard Munro a confidential memorandum in which he strongly recommended a strategic consolidation with Warner. In June 1988, Nicholas and Munro sent to each outside director a copy of the "comprehensive long-term planning document" prepared by the committee of Time executives that had been examining strategies for the 1990s. The memo included reference to and a description of Warner as a potential acquisition candidate.

Thereafter, Munro and Nicholas held meetings with Time's outside directors to discuss, generally, long-term strategies for Time and, specifically, a combination with Warner. Nearly a year later, Time's board reached the point of serious discussion of the "nuts and bolts" of a consolidation with an entertainment company. On July 21, 1988, Time's board met, with all outside directors present. The meeting's purpose was to consider Time's expansion into the entertainment industry on a global scale. Management presented the board with a profile of various

---

[1] The primary concern of Time's outside directors was the preservation of the "Time Culture." They believed that Time had become recognized in this country as an institution built upon a foundation of journalistic integrity. Time's management made a studious effort to refrain from involvement in Time's editorial policy. Several of Time's outside directors feared that a merger with an entertainment company would divert Time's focus from news journalism and threaten the Time Culture. [Editor's note: this and the other footnotes throughout the opinion have been renumbered for the sake of convenience.]

entertainment companies in addition to Warner, including Disney, 20th Century Fox, Universal, and Paramount.

Without any definitive decision on choice of a company, the board approved in principle a strategic plan for Time's expansion. The board gave management the "go-ahead" to continue discussions with Warner concerning the possibility of a merger. With the exception of Temple and Luce, most of the outside directors agreed that a merger involving expansion into the entertainment field promised great growth opportunity for Time. . . .

The board's consensus was that a merger of Time and Warner was feasible, but only if Time controlled the board of the resulting corporation and thereby preserved a management committed to Time's journalistic integrity. To accomplish this goal, the board stressed the importance of carefully defining in advance the corporate governance provisions that would control the resulting entity. Some board members expressed concern over whether such a business combination would place Time "*in play.*" The board discussed the wisdom of adopting further defensive measures to lessen such a possibility.[2]

Of a wide range of companies considered by Time's board as possible merger candidates, Warner Brothers, Paramount, Columbia, M.C.A., Fox, MGM, Disney, and Orion, the board, in July 1988, concluded that Warner was the superior candidate for a consolidation. . . . Warner had just acquired Lorimar and its film studios. Time–Warner could make movies and television shows for use on HBO. Warner had an international distribution system, which Time could use to sell films, videos, books and magazines. Warner was a giant in the music and recording business, an area into which Time wanted to expand. None of the other companies considered had the musical clout of Warner. Time and Warner's cable systems were compatible and could be easily integrated; none of the other companies considered presented such a compatible cable partner. Together, Time and Warner would control half of New York City's cable system; Warner had cable systems in Brooklyn and Queens; and Time controlled cable systems in Manhattan and Queens. Warner's publishing company would integrate well with Time's established publishing company. Time sells hardcover books and magazines, and Warner sells softcover books and comics. Time–Warner could sell all of these publications and Warner's videos by using Time's direct mailing network and Warner's international distribution system. Time's network could be used to promote and merchandise Warner's movies.

---

[2] Time had in place a panoply of defensive devices, including a staggered board, a "poison pill" preferred stock rights plan triggered by an acquisition of 15% of the company, a fifty-day notice period for shareholder motions, and restrictions on shareholders' ability to call a meeting or act by consent.

In August 1988, Levin, Nicholas, and Munro, acting on instructions from Time's board, continued to explore a business combination with Warner. By letter dated August 4, 1988, management informed the outside directors of proposed corporate governance provisions to be discussed with Warner. The provisions incorporated the recommendations of several of Time's outside directors.

From the outset, Time's board favored an all-cash or cash and securities acquisition of Warner as the basis for consolidation. Bruce Wasserstein, Time's financial advisor, also favored an outright purchase of Warner. However, Steve Ross, Warner's CEO, was adamant that a business combination was only practicable on a stock-for-stock basis. Warner insisted on a stock swap in order to preserve its shareholders' equity in the resulting corporation. Time's officers, on the other hand, made it abundantly clear that Time would be the acquiring corporation and that Time would control the resulting board. Time refused to permit itself to be cast as the "acquired" company.

Eventually Time acquiesced in Warner's insistence on a stock-for-stock deal, but talks broke down over corporate governance issues. Time wanted Ross' position as a co-CEO to be temporary and wanted Ross to retire in five years. Ross, however, refused to set a time for his retirement and viewed Time's proposal as indicating a lack of confidence in his leadership. Warner considered it vital that their executives and creative staff not perceive Warner as selling out to Time. Time's request of a guarantee that Time would dominate the CEO succession was objected to as inconsistent with the concept of a Time–Warner merger "of equals." Negotiations ended when the parties reached an impasse. Time's board refused to compromise on its position on corporate governance. Time, and particularly its outside directors, viewed the corporate governance provisions as critical for preserving the "Time Culture" through a pro-Time management at the top.

Throughout the fall of 1988 Time pursued its plan of expansion into the entertainment field; Time held informal discussions with several companies, including Paramount. Capital Cities/ABC approached Time to propose a merger. Talks terminated, however, when Capital Cities/ABC suggested that it was interested in purchasing Time or in controlling the resulting board. Time steadfastly maintained it was not placing itself up for sale.

Warner and Time resumed negotiations in January 1989. The catalyst for the resumption of talks was a private dinner between Steve Ross and Time outside director, Michael Dingman. Dingman was able to convince Ross that the transitional nature of the proposed co-CEO arrangement did not reflect a lack of confidence in Ross. Ross agreed that this course was best for the company and a meeting between Ross and Munro resulted. Ross agreed to retire in five years and let Nicholas succeed him. Negotiations resumed and many of the details of the original stock-for-stock exchange agreement remained intact. In addition, Time's senior management agreed to long-term contracts.

Time insider directors Levin and Nicholas met with Warner's financial advisors to decide upon a stock exchange ratio. Time's board had recognized the potential need to pay a premium in the stock ratio in exchange for dictating the governing arrangement of the new Time–Warner. Levin and outside director Finkelstein were the primary proponents of paying a premium to protect the "Time Culture." The board discussed premium rates of 10%, 15% and 20%. Wasserstein also suggested paying a premium for Warner due to Warner's rapid growth rate. The market exchange ratio of Time stock for Warner stock was .38 in favor of Warner. Warner's financial advisors informed its board that any exchange rate over .400 was a fair deal and any exchange rate over .450 was "one hell of a deal." The parties ultimately agreed upon an exchange rate favoring Warner of .465. On that basis, Warner stockholders would have owned approximately 62% of the common stock of Time–Warner.

On March 3, 1989, Time's board, with all but one director in attendance, met and unanimously approved the stock-for-stock merger with Warner. Warner's board likewise approved the merger. The agreement called for Warner to be merged into a wholly-owned Time subsidiary with Warner becoming the surviving corporation. The common stock of Warner would then be converted into common stock of Time at the agreed upon ratio. Thereafter, the name of Time would be changed to Time–Warner, Inc.

The rules of the New York Stock Exchange required that Time's issuance of shares to effectuate the merger be approved by a vote of Time's stockholders. The Delaware General Corporation Law required approval of the merger by a majority of the Warner stockholders. Delaware law did not require any vote by Time stockholders. The Chancellor concluded that the agreement was the product of "an arms-length negotiation between two parties seeking individual advantage through mutual action."

The resulting company would have a 24–member board, with 12 members representing each corporation. The company would have co-CEO's, at first Ross and Munro, then Ross and Nicholas, and finally, after Ross' retirement, by Nicholas alone. The board would create an editorial committee with a majority of members representing Time. A similar entertainment committee would be controlled by Warner board members. A two-thirds supermajority vote was required to alter CEO successions but an earlier proposal to have supermajority protection for the editorial committee was abandoned. Warner's board suggested raising the compensation levels for Time's senior management under the new corporation. Warner's management, as with most entertainment executives, received higher salaries than comparable executives in news journalism. Time's board, however, rejected Warner's proposal to equalize the salaries of the two management teams.

At its March 3, 1989 meeting, Time's board adopted several defensive tactics. Time entered an automatic share exchange agreement with Warner. Time would receive 17,292,747 shares of Warner's outstanding common stock (9.4%) and Warner would receive 7,080,016 shares of Time's outstanding common stock (11.1%). Either party could trigger the exchange. Time sought out and paid for "confidence" letters from various banks with which it did business. In these letters, the banks promised not to finance any third-party attempt to acquire Time. Time argues these agreements served only to preserve the confidential relationship between itself and the banks. The Chancellor found these agreements to be inconsequential and futile attempts to "dry up" money for a hostile takeover. Time also agreed to a "no-shop" clause, preventing Time from considering any other consolidation proposal, thus relinquishing its power to consider other proposals, regardless of their merits. Time did so at Warner's insistence. Warner did not want to be left "on the auction block" for an unfriendly suitor, if Time were to withdraw from the deal.

Time's board simultaneously established a special committee of outside directors, Finkelstein, Kearns, and Opel, to oversee the merger. The committee's assignment was to resolve any impediments that might arise in the course of working out the details of the merger and its consummation.

Time representatives lauded the lack of debt to the United States Senate and to the President of the United States. Public reaction to the announcement of the merger was positive. Time–Warner would be a media colossus with international scope. The board scheduled the stockholder vote for June 23; and a May 1 record date was set. On May 24, 1989, Time sent out extensive proxy statements to the stockholders regarding the approval vote on the merger. In the meantime, with the merger proceeding without impediment, the special committee had concluded, shortly after its creation, that it was not necessary either to retain independent consultants, legal or financial, or even to meet. Time's board was unanimously in favor of the proposed merger with Warner; and, by the end of May, the Time–Warner merger appeared to be an accomplished fact.

On June 7, 1989, these wishful assumptions were shattered by Paramount's surprising announcement of its all-cash offer to purchase all outstanding shares of Time for $175 per share. The following day, June 8, the trading price of Time's stock rose from $126 to $170 per share. Paramount's offer was said to be "fully negotiable."

Time found Paramount's "fully negotiable" offer to be in fact subject to at least three conditions. First, Time had to terminate its merger agreement and stock exchange agreement with Warner, and remove certain other of its defensive devices, including the redemption of Time's shareholder rights. Second, Paramount had to obtain the required cable franchise transfers from Time in a fashion acceptable to Paramount in its sole discretion. Finally, the offer depended upon a judicial determination that section 203 of the General Corporate Law of Delaware (The Delaware Anti–Takeover Statute) was inapplicable to any Time–Paramount merger. While Paramount's board had been privately advised that it could take months, perhaps over a year, to forge and consummate the deal, Paramount's board publicly proclaimed its ability to close the offer by July 5, 1989. Paramount executives later conceded that none of its directors believed that July 5th was a realistic date to close the transaction.

On June 8, 1989, Time formally responded to Paramount's offer. Time's chairman and CEO, J. Richard Munro, sent an aggressively worded letter to Paramount's CEO, Martin Davis. Munro's letter attacked Davis' personal integrity and called Paramount's offer "smoke and mirrors." Time's nonmanagement directors were not shown the letter before it was sent. However, at a board meeting that same day, all members endorsed management's response as well as the letter's content.

Over the following eight days, Time's board met three times to discuss Paramount's $175 offer. The board viewed Paramount's offer as inadequate and concluded that its proposed merger with Warner was the better course of action. Therefore, the board declined to open any negotiations with Paramount and held steady its course toward a merger with Warner.

In June, Time's board of directors met several times. During the course of their June meetings, Time's outside directors met frequently without management, officers or directors being present. At the request of the outside directors, corporate counsel was present during the board meetings and, from time to time, the management directors were asked to leave the board sessions. During the course of these meetings, Time's financial advisors informed the board that, on an auction basis, Time's per share value was materially higher than [Paramount]'s $175 per share offer. After this advice, the board concluded that Paramount's $175 offer was inadequate.

At these June meetings, certain Time directors expressed their concern that Time stockholders would not comprehend the long-term benefits of the Warner merger. Large quantities of Time shares were held by institutional investors. The board feared that even though there appeared to be wide support for the Warner transaction, Paramount's cash premium would be a tempting prospect to these investors. In mid-June, Time sought permission from the New York Stock Exchange to alter its rules and allow the Time–Warner merger to proceed without stockholder approval. Time did so at Warner's insistence. The New York Stock Exchange rejected Time's request on June 15; and on that day, the value of Time stock reached $182 per share.

The following day, June 16, Time's board met to take up Paramount's offer. The board's prevailing belief was that Paramount's bid posed a threat to Time's control of its own destiny and retention of the "Time Culture." Even after Time's financial advisors made another presentation of Paramount and its business attributes, Time's board maintained its position that a combination with Warner offered greater potential for Time. Warner provided Time a much desired production capability and an established international marketing chain. Time's advisors suggested various options, including defensive measures. The board considered and rejected the idea of purchasing Paramount in a "Pac Man" defense.[3] The board considered other defenses, including a recapitalization, the acquisition of another company, and a material change in the present capitalization structure or dividend policy. The board determined to retain its same advisors even in light of the changed circumstances. The board rescinded its agreement to pay its advisors a bonus based on the consummation of the Time–Warner merger and agreed to pay a flat fee for any advice rendered. Finally, Time's board formally rejected Paramount's offer.

At the same meeting, Time's board decided to recast its consolidation with Warner into an outright cash and securities acquisition of Warner by Time; and Time so informed Warner. Time accordingly restructured its proposal to acquire Warner as follows: Time would make an immediate all-cash offer for 51% of Warner's outstanding stock at $70 per share. The remaining 49% would be purchased at some later date for a mixture of cash and securities worth $70 per share. To provide the funds required for its outright acquisition of Warner, Time would assume 7–10 billion dollars worth of debt, thus eliminating one of the principal transaction-related benefits of the original merger agreement. Nine billion dollars of the total purchase price would be allocated to the purchase of Warner's goodwill.

Warner agreed but insisted on certain terms. Warner sought a control premium and guarantees that the governance provisions found in the original merger agreement would remain intact. Warner further sought agreements that Time would not employ its poison pill against Warner and that, unless enjoined, Time would be legally bound to complete the transaction. Time's board agreed to these last measures only at the insistence of Warner. For its part, Time was assured of its ability

---

[3] In a "Pac Man" defense, Time would launch a tender offer for the stock of Paramount, thus consuming its rival. *Moran v. Household Intern., Inc.*, Del.Supr., 500 A.2d 1346, 1350 n. 6 (1985).

to extend its efforts into production areas and international markets, all the while maintaining the Time identity and culture. The Chancellor found the initial Time–Warner transaction to have been negotiated at arms length and the restructured Time–Warner transaction to have resulted from Paramount's offer and its expected effect on a Time shareholder vote.

On June 23, 1989, Paramount raised its all-cash offer to buy Time's outstanding stock to $200 per share. Paramount still professed that all aspects of the offer were negotiable. Time's board met on June 26, 1989 and formally rejected Paramount's $200 per share second offer. The board reiterated its belief that, despite the $25 increase, the offer was still inadequate. The Time board maintained that the Warner transaction offered a greater long-term value for the stockholders and, unlike Paramount's offer, did not pose a threat to Time's survival and its "culture." Paramount then filed this action in the Court of Chancery.

II

The Shareholder Plaintiffs first assert a *Revlon* claim. They contend that the March 4 Time–Warner agreement effectively put Time up for sale, triggering *Revlon* duties, requiring Time's board to enhance short-term shareholder value and to treat all other interested acquirors on an equal basis. The Shareholder Plaintiffs base this argument on two facts: (i) the ultimate Time–Warner exchange ratio of .465 favoring Warner, resulting in Warner shareholders' receipt of 62% of the combined company; and (ii) the subjective intent of Time's directors as evidenced in their statements that the market might perceive the Time–Warner merger as putting Time up "for sale" and their adoption of various defensive measures.

The Shareholder Plaintiffs further contend that Time's directors, in structuring the original merger transaction to be "takeover-proof," triggered *Revlon* duties by foreclosing their shareholders from any prospect of obtaining a control premium. In short, plaintiffs argue that Time's board's decision to merge with Warner imposed a fiduciary duty to maximize immediate share value and not erect unreasonable barriers to further bids. Therefore, they argue, the Chancellor erred in finding: that Paramount's bid for Time did not place Time "for sale"; that Time's transaction with Warner did not result in any transfer of control; and that the combined Time–Warner was not so large as to preclude the possibility of the stockholders of Time–Warner receiving a future control premium.

Paramount asserts only a *Unocal* claim in which the shareholder plaintiffs join. Paramount contends that the Chancellor, in applying the first part of the *Unocal* test, erred in finding that Time's board had reasonable grounds to believe that Paramount posed both a legally cognizable threat to Time shareholders and a danger to Time's corporate policy and effectiveness. Paramount also contests the court's finding that Time's board made a reasonable and objective investigation of Paramount's offer so as to be informed before rejecting it. Paramount further claims that the court erred in applying *Unocal* 's second part in finding Time's response to be "reasonable." Paramount points primarily to the preclusive effect of the revised agreement which denied Time shareholders the opportunity both to vote on the agreement and to respond to Paramount's tender offer. Paramount argues that the underlying motivation of Time's board in adopting these defensive measures was management's desire to perpetuate itself in office.

The Court of Chancery posed the pivotal question presented by this case to be: Under what circumstances must a board of directors abandon an in-place plan of corporate development in order to provide its shareholders with the option to elect and realize an immediate control premium? As applied to this case, the question becomes: Did Time's board, having developed a strategic plan of global expansion to be launched through a business combination with Warner, come under a fiduciary duty to jettison its plan and put the corporation's future in the hands of its shareholders?

While we affirm the result reached by the Chancellor, we think it unwise to place undue emphasis upon long-term versus short-term corporate strategy. Two key predicates underpin our analysis. First, Delaware law imposes on a board of directors the duty to manage the business and affairs of the corporation. . . . This broad mandate includes a conferred authority to set a corporate course of action, including time frame, designed to enhance corporate profitability. Thus, the question of "long-term" versus "short-term" values is largely irrelevant because directors, generally, are obliged to chart a course for a corporation which is in its best interests without regard to a fixed investment horizon. Second, absent a limited set of circumstances as defined under *Revlon,* a board of directors, while always required to act in an informed manner, is not under any *per se* duty to maximize shareholder value in the short term, even in the context of a takeover. In our view, the pivotal question presented by this case is: "Did Time, by entering into the proposed merger with Warner, put itself up for sale?" A resolution of that issue through application of *Revlon* has a significant bearing upon the resolution of the derivative *Unocal* issue.

A.

We first take up plaintiffs' principal *Revlon* argument, summarized above. In rejecting this argument, the Chancellor found the original Time–Warner merger agreement not to constitute a "change of control" and concluded that the transaction did not trigger *Revlon* duties. The Chancellor's conclusion is premised on a finding that "[b]efore the merger agreement was signed, control of the corporation existed in a fluid aggregation of unaffiliated shareholders representing a voting majority—in other words, in the market." The Chancellor's findings of fact are supported by the record and his conclusion is correct as a matter of law. However, we premise our rejection of plaintiffs' *Revlon* claim on different grounds, namely, the absence of any substantial evidence to conclude that Time's board, in negotiating with Warner, made the dissolution or break-up of the corporate entity inevitable, as was the case in *Revlon*.

Under Delaware law there are, generally speaking and without excluding other possibilities, two circumstances which may implicate *Revlon* duties. The first, and clearer one, is when a corporation initiates an active bidding process seeking to sell itself or to effect a business reorganization involving a clear break-up of the company. . . . However, *Revlon* duties may also be triggered where, in response to a bidder's offer, a target abandons its long-term strategy and seeks an alternative transaction involving the breakup of the company. Thus, in *Revlon,* when the board responded to Pantry Pride's offer by contemplating a "bust-up" sale of assets in a leveraged acquisition, we imposed upon the board a duty to maximize immediate shareholder value and an obligation to auction the company fairly. If, however, the board's reaction to a hostile tender offer is found to constitute only a defensive response and not an abandonment of the corporation's continued existence, *Revlon* duties are not triggered, though *Unocal* duties attach. . . .

The plaintiffs insist that even though the original Time–Warner agreement may not have worked "an objective change of control," the transaction made a "sale" of Time inevitable. Plaintiffs rely on the subjective intent of Time's board of directors and principally upon certain board members' expressions of concern that the Warner transaction *might* be viewed as effectively putting Time up for sale. Plaintiffs argue that the use of a lock-up agreement, a no-shop clause, and so-called "dry-up" agreements prevented shareholders from obtaining a control premium in the immediate future and thus violated *Revlon*.

We agree with the Chancellor that such evidence is entirely insufficient to invoke *Revlon* duties; and we decline to extend *Revlon's* application to corporate transactions simply because they might be construed as putting a corporation either "in play" or "up for sale." . . . The adoption of structural safety devices alone does not trigger *Revlon*. Rather, as the Chancellor stated, such devices are properly subject to a *Unocal* analysis.

Finally, we do not find in Time's recasting of its merger agreement with Warner from a share exchange to a share purchase a basis to conclude that Time had either abandoned its strategic plan or made a sale of Time inevitable. The Chancellor found that although the merged Time–Warner company would be large (with a value approaching approximately $30 billion), recent takeover cases have proven that acquisition of the combined company might nonetheless be possible. . . . The legal consequence is that *Unocal* alone applies to determine whether the business judgment rule attaches to the revised agreement. . . .

B.

We turn now to plaintiffs' *Unocal* claim. We begin by noting, as did the Chancellor, that our decision does not require us to pass on the wisdom of the board's decision to enter into the original Time–Warner agreement. That is not a court's task. Our task is simply to review the record to determine whether there is sufficient evidence to support the Chancellor's conclusion that the initial Time–Warner agreement was the product of a proper exercise of business judgment. . . .

We have purposely detailed the evidence of the Time board's deliberative approach, beginning in 1983–84, to expand itself. Time's decision in 1988 to combine with Warner was made only after what could be fairly characterized as an exhaustive appraisal of Time's future as a corporation. After concluding in 1983–84 that the corporation must expand to survive, and beyond journalism into entertainment, the board combed the field of available entertainment companies. By 1987 Time had focused upon Warner; by late July 1988 Time's board was convinced that Warner would provide the best "fit" for Time to achieve its strategic objectives. The record attests to the zealousness of Time's executives, fully supported by their directors, in seeing to the preservation of Time's "culture," i.e., its perceived editorial integrity in journalism. We find ample evidence in the record to support the Chancellor's conclusion that the Time board's decision to expand the business of the company through its March 3 merger with Warner was entitled to the protection of the business judgment rule. *See Aronson v. Lewis*, Del.Supr., 473 A.2d 805, 812 (1984).

The Chancellor reached a different conclusion in addressing the Time–Warner transaction as revised three months later. He found that the revised agreement was defense-motivated and designed to avoid the potentially disruptive effect that Paramount's offer would have had on consummation of the proposed merger were it put to a shareholder vote. Thus, the court declined to apply the traditional business judgment rule to the revised transaction and instead analyzed the Time board's June 16 decision under *Unocal*. The court ruled that *Unocal* applied to all director actions taken, following receipt of Paramount's hostile tender offer, that were reasonably determined to be defensive. Clearly that was a correct ruling and no party disputes that ruling.

In *Unocal,* we held that before the business judgment rule is applied to a board's adoption of a defensive measure, the burden will lie with the board to prove (a) reasonable grounds for believing that a danger to corporate policy and effectiveness existed; and (b) that the defensive measure adopted was reasonable in relation to the threat posed. *Unocal,* 493 A.2d 946. Directors satisfy the first part of the *Unocal* test by demonstrating good faith and reasonable investigation. We have repeatedly stated that the refusal to entertain an offer may comport with a valid exercise of a board's business judgment. . . .

Unocal involved a two-tier, highly coercive tender offer. In such a case, the threat is obvious: shareholders may be compelled to tender to avoid being treated adversely in the second stage of the transaction. In subsequent cases, the Court of Chancery has suggested that an all-cash, all-shares offer, falling within a range of values that a shareholder might reasonably prefer, cannot constitute a legally recognized "threat" to shareholder interests sufficient to withstand a *Unocal* analysis. . . . In those cases, the Court of Chancery determined that whatever threat existed related only to the shareholders and only to price and not to the corporation.

From those decisions by our Court of Chancery, Paramount and the individual plaintiffs extrapolate a rule of law that an all-cash, all-shares offer with values reasonably in the range of acceptable price cannot pose any objective threat to a corporation or its shareholders. Thus, Paramount would have us hold that only if the value of Paramount's offer were determined to be clearly inferior to the value created by management's plan to merge with Warner could the offer be viewed— objectively—as a threat.

Implicit in the plaintiffs' argument is the view that a hostile tender offer can pose only two types of threats: the threat of coercion that results from a two-tier offer promising unequal treatment for nontendering shareholders; and the threat of inadequate value from an all-shares, all-cash offer at a price below what a target board in good faith deems to be the present value of its shares. . . . Since Paramount's offer was all-cash, the only conceivable "threat," plaintiffs argue, was inadequate value.[4] We

---

[4] Some commentators have suggested that the threats posed by hostile offers be categorized into not two but three types: "(i) *opportunity loss* ... [where] a hostile offer might deprive target shareholders of the opportunity to select a superior alternative offered by target management [or, we would add, offered by another bidder]; (ii) *structural coercion,* ... the risk that disparate treatment of non-tendering shareholders might distort shareholders' tender decisions; and ... (iii) *substantive coercion,* ... the risk that shareholders will mistakenly accept an underpriced offer because they disbelieve management's representations of intrinsic value." The recognition of substantive coercion, the authors suggest, would help guarantee that the *Unocal* standard becomes an effective intermediate standard of review. Gilson & Kraakman, *Delaware's*

disapprove of such a narrow and rigid construction of *Unocal,* for the reasons which follow.

Plaintiffs' position represents a fundamental misconception of our standard of review under *Unocal* principally because it would involve the court in substituting its judgment as to what is a "better" deal for that of a corporation's board of directors. . . .

The usefulness of *Unocal* as an analytical tool is precisely its flexibility in the face of a variety of fact scenarios. *Unocal* is not intended as an abstract standard; neither is it a structured and mechanistic procedure of appraisal. Thus, we have said that directors may consider, when evaluating the threat posed by a takeover bid, the "inadequacy of the price offered, nature and timing of the offer, questions of illegality, the impact on 'constituencies' other than shareholders . . . the risk of nonconsummation, and the quality of securities being offered in the exchange." 493 A.2d at 955. The open-ended analysis mandated by *Unocal* is not intended to lead to a simple mathematical exercise: that is, of comparing the discounted value of Time–Warner's expected trading price at some future date with Paramount's offer and determining which is the higher. Indeed, in our view, precepts underlying the business judgment rule militate against a court's engaging in the process of attempting to appraise and evaluate the relative merits of a long-term versus a short-term investment goal for shareholders. To engage in such an exercise is a distortion of the *Unocal* process and, in particular, the application of the second part of *Unocal*'s test, discussed below.

In this case, the Time board reasonably determined that inadequate value was not the only legally cognizable threat that Paramount's all-cash, all-shares offer could present. Time's board concluded that Paramount's eleventh hour offer posed other threats. One concern was that Time shareholders might elect to tender into Paramount's cash offer in ignorance or a mistaken belief of the strategic benefit which a business combination with Warner might produce. Moreover, Time viewed the conditions attached to Paramount's offer as introducing a degree of uncertainty that skewed a comparative analysis. Further, the timing of Paramount's offer to follow issuance of Time's proxy notice was viewed as arguably designed to upset, if not confuse, the Time stockholders' vote. Given this record evidence, we cannot conclude that the Time board's decision of June 6 that Paramount's offer posed a threat to corporate policy and effectiveness was lacking in good faith or dominated by motives of either entrenchment or self-interest.

Paramount also contends that the Time board had not duly investigated Paramount's offer. Therefore, Paramount argues, Time was unable to make an informed decision that the offer posed a threat to

Time's corporate policy. Although the Chancellor did not address this issue directly, his findings of fact do detail Time's exploration of the available entertainment companies, including Paramount, before determining that Warner provided the best strategic "fit." In addition, the court found that Time's board rejected Paramount's offer because Paramount did not serve Time's objectives or meet Time's needs. Thus, the record does, in our judgment, demonstrate that Time's board was adequately informed of the potential benefits of a transaction with Paramount. We agree with the Chancellor that the Time board's lengthy pre-June investigation of potential merger candidates, including Paramount, mooted any obligation on Time's part to halt its merger process with Warner to reconsider Paramount. Time's board was under no obligation to negotiate with Paramount. . . . Time's failure to negotiate cannot be fairly found to have been uninformed. The evidence supporting this finding is materially enhanced by the fact that twelve of Time's sixteen board members were outside independent directors. . . .

We turn to the second part of the *Unocal* analysis. The obvious requisite to determining the reasonableness of a defensive action is a clear identification of the nature of the threat. As the Chancellor correctly noted, this "requires an evaluation of the importance of the corporate objective threatened; alternative methods of protecting that objective; impacts of the 'defensive' action, and other relevant factors." . . . It is not until both parts of the *Unocal* inquiry have been satisfied that the business judgment rule attaches to defensive actions of a board of directors. *Unocal,* 493 A.2d at 954. As applied to the facts of this case, the question is whether the record evidence supports the Court of Chancery's conclusion that the restructuring of the Time–Warner transaction, including the adoption of several preclusive defensive measures, was a *reasonable response* in relation to a perceived threat.

Paramount argues that, assuming its tender offer posed a threat, Time's response was unreasonable in precluding Time's shareholders from accepting the tender offer or receiving a control premium in the immediately foreseeable future. Once again, the contention stems, we believe, from a fundamental misunderstanding of where the power of corporate governance lies. Delaware law confers the management of the corporate enterprise to the stockholders' duly elected board representatives. 8 *Del.C.* § 141(a). The fiduciary duty to manage a corporate enterprise includes the selection of a time frame for achievement of corporate goals. That duty may not be delegated to the stockholders. Directors are not obliged to abandon a deliberately conceived corporate plan for a short-term shareholder profit unless there is clearly no basis to sustain the corporate strategy. *See, e.g., Revlon,* 506 A.2d 173.

Although the Chancellor blurred somewhat the discrete analyses required under *Unocal,* he did conclude that Time's board reasonably perceived Paramount's offer to be a significant threat to the planned Time–Warner merger and that Time's response was not "overly broad." We have found that even in light of a valid threat, management actions that are coercive in nature or force upon shareholders a management-sponsored alternative to a hostile offer may be struck down as unreasonable and nonproportionate responses. . . .

Here, on the record facts, the Chancellor found that Time's responsive action to Paramount's tender offer was not aimed at "cramming down" on its shareholders a management-sponsored alternative, but rather had as its goal the carrying forward of a pre-existing transaction in an altered form. Thus, the response was reasonably related to the threat. The Chancellor noted that the revised agreement and its accompanying safety devices did not preclude Paramount from making an offer for the combined Time–Warner company or from changing the conditions of its offer so as not to make the offer dependent upon the nullification of the Time–Warner agreement. Thus, the response was proportionate. We affirm the Chancellor's rulings as clearly supported by the record. Finally, we note that although Time was required, as a result of Paramount's hostile offer, to incur a heavy debt to finance its acquisition of Warner, that fact alone does not render the board's decision unreasonable so long as the directors could reasonably perceive the debt load not to be so injurious to the corporation as to jeopardize its well being.

C.

Conclusion

Applying the test for grant or denial of preliminary injunctive relief, we find plaintiffs failed to establish a reasonable likelihood of ultimate success on the merits. Therefore, we affirm.

NOTES AND QUESTIONS

1. What Do You Think? Hostile takeover cases are some of the most exciting and colorful in all of business organizations law. They also have some of the most far-reaching effects for shareholders. That said, if you were a Time shareholder, how would you feel about this deal and decision? Would you want a chance to accept Paramount's offer of $200 per share?

Does it affect your decision to note that by July 25, 1990, Time shares had declined in the market to $93 a share? And, the carnage doesn't end there. The combined Time-Warner eventually merged with America Online in what is widely regarded as one of the most disastrous mergers in history. All said and done, "[i]f you were a shareholder of Time back in 1989 and held your shares through various splits over the years, they would now be worth $113.76 each, about where they were trading more than 14 years ago and far below the Paramount offer. Meanwhile, if you'd just bought the stocks in the S&P 500 index, you would have almost tripled your money." Steven Rattner, *Merge at Your Own Risk*, WALL ST. J., Jul. 30, 2003, at A13.

What do you think? If you were a Time shareholder as described above, would you be happy with the preservation of the "Time" culture at this price? Did the Time board of directors blow it here? Did the Delaware Supreme Court?

_____

_____

_____

_____

_____

2. The Specter of a Conflict. Normally, as we have seen, the decisions of a board of directors are protected from judicial scrutiny by the business judgment rule. However, in cases where there is a conflict of interest, the protections of the business judgment rule do not apply and the burden is shifted to the directors to prove that the transaction is intrinsically fair. The reason for this is that, in cases of conflicts of interest, the justifications for the business judgment rule, as discussed herein, do not exist.

In takeover cases, the Delaware Supreme Court has noted that, while perhaps not a full-blown conflict of interest, "when a board implements anti-takeover measures there arises 'the omnipresent specter that a board may be acting primarily in its own interests, rather than those of the corporation and its shareholders . . .' *Revlon, Inc. v. MacAndrews & Forbes Holdings, Inc.*, 506 A.2d 173, 180 (Del. 1986) (*quoting Unocal Corp. v. Mesa Petroleum Co.*, 493 A.2d 946, 954 (Del. 1985). Thus, as described in *Time*, the courts apply a somewhat more exacting standard of analysis in takeover cases. What interests of the directors is the court concerned about? Or, to put it another way, what normally happens to directors and officers of a company that is taken over by another company? Do they normally keep their jobs?

That said, why do you think the courts apply a more lenient standard in these situations? Is it because mergers and takeovers can often be very valuable to shareholders and a good thing for the economy? Is the specter of a conflict that managers might just want to entrench themselves at the cost of the shareholders any less of a conflict than the more run-of-the-mill conflict transactions?

_____

_____

_____

_____

_____

_____

3. Faithful Directors (Stewards)? Do you think the members of the Time board were faithful in exercising their duties as directors? The position of a steward is quite analogous to the position of a director or manager. Read *Luke* 16:1-13 and 1 *Corinthians* 4:1-2. Are the motivations of the Time directors more akin to those of the Unrighteous Steward or the Apostle Paul? If it is the Unrighteous Steward, then what should the standard be by which anti-takeover measures are judged?

_____

_____

_____

_____

_____

_____

CHAPTER 8
IS INSIDER TRADING WRONG?

Securities and Exchange Commission v. Cuban
620 F.3d 551 (5th Cir. 2010)

This case raises questions of the scope of liability under the misappropriation theory of insider trading. Taking a different view from our able district court brother of the allegations of the complaint, we are persuaded that the case should not have been dismissed under Fed.R.Civ.P. 9(b) and 12 and must proceed to discovery.

Mark Cuban is a well known entrepreneur and current owner of the Dallas Mavericks and Landmark theaters, among other businesses. The SEC brought this suit against Cuban alleging he violated . . . Section 10(b) of the Securities Exchange Act of 1934 and Rule 10b–5 by trading in Mamma.com stock in breach of his duty to the CEO and Mamma.com—amounting to insider trading under the misappropriation theory of liability. The core allegation is that Cuban received confidential information from the CEO of Mamma.com, a Canadian search engine company in which Cuban was a large minority stakeholder, agreed to keep the information confidential, and acknowledged he could not trade on the information. The SEC alleges that, armed with the inside information regarding a private investment of public equity (PIPE) offering, Cuban sold his stake in the company in an effort to avoid losses from the inevitable fall in Mamma.com's share price when the offering was announced. Cuban moved to dismiss the action . . . . The district court found that, at most, the complaint alleged an agreement to keep the information confidential, but did not include an agreement not to trade. Finding a simple confidentiality agreement to be insufficient to create a duty to disclose or abstain from trading under the securities laws, the court granted Cuban's motion to dismiss. The SEC appeals, arguing that a confidentiality agreement creates a duty to disclose or abstain and that, regardless, the confidentiality agreement alleged in the complaint also contained an agreement not to trade on the information and that agreement would create such a duty.

We review de novo the district court's dismissal for failure to state a claim under Rule 12(b)(6). We accept "all well pleaded facts as true, viewing them in the light most favorable to the plaintiff." The "'complaint must contain sufficient factual matter', accepted as true, to 'state a claim to relief that is plausible on its face.'" "'Factual allegations must be enough to raise a right to relief above the speculative level, on the assumption that all the allegations in the complaint are true (even if doubtful in fact).'"

The SEC alleges that Cuban's trading constituted insider trading and violated Section 10(b) of the Securities Exchange Act. Section 10(b) makes it

> unlawful for any person, directly or indirectly, by the use of any means or instrumentality of interstate commerce or of the mails, or of any facility of any national securities exchange ... [t]o use or employ, in connection with the purchase or sale of any security ... any manipulative or deceptive device or contrivance in contravention of such rules and regulations as the Commission may prescribe as necessary or appropriate in the public interest or for the protection of investors.

Pursuant to this section, the SEC promulgated Rule 10b–5, which makes it unlawful to

> (a) To employ any device, scheme, or artifice to defraud,
> (b) To make any untrue statement of a material fact or to omit to state a material fact necessary in order to make the statements made, in the light of the circumstances under which they were made, not misleading, or
> (c) To engage in any act, practice, or course of business which operates or would operate as a fraud or deceit upon any person, in connection with the purchase or sale of any security.

The Supreme Court has interpreted section 10(b) to prohibit insider trading under two complementary theories, the "classical theory" and the "misappropriation theory."

The classical theory of insider trading prohibits a "corporate insider" from trading on material nonpublic information obtained from his position within the corporation without disclosing the information. According to this theory, there exists "a relationship of trust and confidence between the shareholders of a corporation and those insiders who have obtained confidential information by reason of their position with that corporation."

[*Chiarella v. United States*, 445 U.S. 222, 228 (1980).] Trading on such confidential information qualifies as a "deceptive device" under section 10(b) because by using that information for his own personal benefit, the corporate insider breaches his duty to the shareholders. The corporate insider is under a duty to "disclose or abstain"—he must tell the shareholders of his knowledge and intention to trade or abstain from trading altogether.

There are at least two important variations of the classical theory of insider trading. The first is that even an individual who does not qualify as a traditional insider may become a "temporary insider" if by entering "into a special confidential relationship in the conduct of the business of the enterprise [they] are given access to information solely for corporate purposes." [*Dirks v. SEC*, 463 U.S. 646, 655 n. 14 (1983).] Thus underwriters, accountants, lawyers, or consultants are all considered corporate insiders when by virtue of their professional relationship with the corporation they are given access to confidential information. The second variation is that an individual who receives information from a corporate insider may be, but is not always, prohibited from trading on that information as a tippee. "[T]he tippee's duty to disclose or abstain is derivative from that of the insider's duty" and the tippee's obligation arises "from his role as a participant after the fact in the insider's breach of a fiduciary duty." [*Id.* at 659.] Crucially, "a tippee assumes a fiduciary duty to the shareholders of a corporation not to trade on material nonpublic information only when the insider has breached his fiduciary duty to the shareholders by disclosing the information to the tippee and the tippee knows or should know there has been a breach." [*Id.* at 660.] The insider breaches his fiduciary duty when he receives a "direct or indirect personal benefit from the disclosure." [*Id.* at 663.]

Both the temporary-insider and tippee twists on the classical theory retain its core principle that the duty to disclose or abstain is derived from the corporate insider's duty to his shareholders. The misappropriation theory does not rest on this duty. It rather holds that a person violates section 10(b) "when he misappropriates confidential information for securities trading purposes, in breach of a duty owed to the source of the information." The Supreme Court first adopted this theory in *United States v. O'Hagan* [521 U.S. 642 (1997)]. There, a lawyer traded the securities of a company his client was targeting for a takeover. O'Hagan could not be liable under the classical theory as he owed no duty to the shareholders of the target company. Nevertheless, the court found O'Hagan violated section 10(b). The Court held that in trading the target company's securities, O'Hagan misappropriated the confidential information regarding the planned corporate takeover, breaching "a duty of trust and confidence" he owed to his law firm and client. Trading on such information "involves feigning fidelity to the source of information and thus utilizes a 'deceptive device' as required by section 10(b)." The Court stated that while there is "no general duty between all participants in market transactions to forgo actions based on material nonpublic information," the breach of a duty to the source of the information is sufficient to give rise to insider trading liability.

While *O'Hagan* did not set the contours of a relationship of "trust and confidence" giving rise to the duty to disclose or abstain and misappropriation liability, we are tasked to determine whether Cuban had such a relationship with Mamma.com. The SEC seeks to rely on Rule 10b5–2(b)(1), which states that a person has "a duty of trust and confidence" for purposes of misappropriation liability when that person "agrees to maintain information in confidence." In dismissing the case, the district court read the complaint to allege that Cuban agreed not to disclose any confidential information but did not agree not to trade, that such a confidentiality agreement was insufficient to create a duty to disclose or abstain from trading under the misappropriation theory, and that the SEC overstepped its authority under section 10(b) in issuing Rule 10b5–2(b)(1). We differ from the district court in reading the complaint and need not reach the latter issues.

The complaint alleges that, in March 2004, Cuban acquired 600,000 shares, a 6.3% stake, of Mamma.com. Later that spring, Mamma.com decided to raise capital through a PIPE offering on the advice of the investment bank Merriman Curhan Ford & Co. At the end of June, at Merriman's suggestion, Mamma.com decided to invite Cuban to participate in the PIPE offering. "The CEO was instructed to contact Cuban and to preface the conversation by informing Cuban that he had confidential information to convey to him in order to make sure that Cuban understood—before the information was conveyed to him—that he would have to keep the information confidential."

After getting in touch with Cuban on June 28, Mamma.com's CEO told Cuban he had confidential information for him and Cuban agreed to keep whatever information the CEO shared confidential. The CEO then told Cuban about the PIPE offering. Cuban became very upset "and said, among other things, that he did not like PIPEs because they dilute the existing shareholders." "At the end of the call, Cuban told the CEO 'Well, now I'm screwed. I can't sell.'"

The CEO told the company's executive chairman about the conversation with Cuban. The executive chairman sent an email to the other Mamma.com board members updating them on the PIPE offering. The executive chairman included:

> Today, after much discussion, [the CEO] spoke to Mark
> Cuban about this equity raise and whether or not he would
> be interested in participating. As anticipated he initially

"flew off the handle" and said he would sell his shares (recognizing that he was not able to do anything until we announce the equity) but then asked to see the terms and conditions which we have arranged for him to receive from one of the participating investor groups with which he has dealt in the past.

The CEO then sent Cuban a follow up email, writing "'[i]f you want more details about the private placement please contact ... [Merriman].'"

Cuban called the Merriman representative and they spoke for eight minutes. "During that call, the salesman supplied Cuban with additional confidential details about the PIPE. In response to Cuban's questions, the salesman told him that the PIPE was being sold at a discount to the market price and that the offering included other incentives for the PIPE investors." It is a plausible inference that Cuban learned the off-market prices available to him and other PIPE participants.

With that information and one minute after speaking with the Merriman representative, Cuban called his broker and instructed him to sell his entire stake in the company. Cuban sold 10,000 shares during the evening of June 28, 2004, and the remainder during regular trading the next day.

That day, the executive chairman sent another email to the board, updating them on the previous day's discussions with Cuban, stating "'we did speak to Mark Cuban ([the CEO] and, subsequently, our investment banker) to find out if he had any interest in participating to the extent of maintaining his interest. His answers were: he would not invest, he does not want the company to make acquisitions, he will sell his shares which he can not do until after we announce.'"

After the markets closed on June 29, Mamma.com announced the PIPE offering. The next day, Mamma.com's stock price fell 8.5% and continued to decline over the next week, eventually closing down 39% from the June 29 closing price. By selling his shares when he did, Cuban avoided over $750,000 in losses. Cuban notified the SEC that he had sold his stake in the company and publically stated that he sold his shares because Mamma.com "was conducting a PIPE, which issued shares at a discount to the prevailing market price and also would have caused his ownership position to be diluted."

In reading the complaint to allege only an agreement of confidentiality, the court held that Cuban's statement that he was "screwed" because he "[could not] sell" "appears to express his belief, at least at that time, that it would be illegal for him to sell his Mamma.com shares based on the information the CEO provided." But the court stated that this statement "cannot reasonably be understood as an agreement not to sell based on the information." The court found "the complaint asserts no facts that reasonably suggest that the CEO intended to obtain from Cuban an agreement to refrain from trading on the information as opposed to an agreement merely to keep it confidential." Finally, the court stated that "the CEO's expectation that Cuban would not sell was also insufficient" to allege any further agreement.

Reading the complaint in the light most favorable to the SEC, we reach a different conclusion. In isolation, the statement "Well, now I'm screwed. I can't sell" can plausibly be read to express Cuban's view that learning the confidences regarding the PIPE forbade his selling his stock before the offering but to express no agreement not to do so. However, after Cuban expressed the view that he could not sell to the CEO, he gained access to the confidences of the PIPE offering. According to the complaint's recounting of the executive chairman's email to the board, during his short conversation with the CEO regarding the planned PIPE offering, Cuban requested the terms and conditions of the offering. Based on this request, the CEO sent Cuban a follow up email providing the contact information for Merriman. Cuban called the salesman, who told Cuban "that the PIPE was being sold at a discount to the market price and that the offering included other incentives for the PIPE investors." Only after Cuban reached out to obtain this additional information, following the statement of his understanding that he could not sell, did Cuban contact his broker and sell his stake in the company. The allegations, taken in their entirety, provide more than a plausible basis to find that the understanding between the CEO and Cuban was that he was not to trade, that it was more than a simple confidentiality agreement. By contacting the sales representative to obtain the pricing information, Cuban was able to evaluate his potential losses or gains from his decision to either participate or refrain from participating in the PIPE offering. It is at least plausible that each of the parties understood, if only implicitly, that Mamma.com would only provide the terms and conditions of the offering to Cuban for the purpose of evaluating whether he would participate in the offering, and that Cuban could not use the information for his own personal benefit. It would require additional facts that have not been put before us for us to conclude that the parties could not plausibly have reached this shared understanding. Under Cuban's reading, he was allowed to trade on the information but prohibited from telling others—in effect providing him an exclusive license to trade on the material nonpublic information. Perhaps this was the understanding, or perhaps Cuban mislead the CEO regarding the timing of his sale in order to obtain a confidential look at the details of the PIPE. We say only that on this factually sparse record, it is at least equally plausible that all sides understood there was to be no trading before the PIPE. That both Cuban and the CEO expressed the belief that Cuban could not trade appears to reinforce the plausibility of this reading.

Given the paucity of jurisprudence on the question of what constitutes a relationship of "trust and confidence" and the inherently fact-bound nature of determining whether such a duty exists, we decline to first determine or place our thumb on the scale in the district court's determination of its presence or to now draw the contours of any liability that it might bring, including the force of Rule 10b5–2(b)(1). Rather, we VACATE the judgment dismissing the case and REMAND to the court of first instance for further proceedings including discovery, consideration of summary judgment, and trial, if reached.

NOTES AND QUESTIONS

1. What Do You Think? Do you think Mark Cuban did anything wrong here? What would you have done in his situation?

———————————————————————————

———————————————————————————

———————————————————————————

———————————————————————————

———————————————————————————

———————————————————————————

2. Insider Trading Theories. The court notes that there are two major theories of insider trading liability. The one primarily at issue in the *SEC v. Cuban* is the misappropriation theory, set forth by the Supreme Court in *US v. O'Hagan.* What is the other one? *See Chiarella v. United States,* 445 U.S. 222 (1980) and *Dirks v. SEC,* 463 U.S. 646 (1983). What must be shown under each of these theories in order to hold the insider liable?

———————————————————————————

———————————————————————————

———————————————————————————

———————————————————————————

———————————————————————————

———————————————————————————

3. Trading in Stocks v. Trading in Land. Imagine that you discover that a certain piece of property is rich with oil reserves. The owner doesn't know that his land contains this valuable resource, and he is therefore willing to sell it to you for much less than if he was aware of the existence of the oil. Do you violate the law by purchasing the land without disclosing the existence of the oil reserves to the owner? *See Matthew* 13:44. Perhaps surprisingly, the answer is no.

Imagine instead that you discover that a publicly traded mineral exploration company has made a particularly lucrative ore strike. This information is not yet public. May you go buy shares of stock in the company knowing that those shares will increase in value substantially once news of the ore strike is made public? *See Securities and Exchange Commission v. Texas Gulf Sulphur Co.*, 401 F.2d 833 (2d cir. 1968), *cert. denied*, 394 U.S. 976 (1969). Does it matter how you found out about the ore strike? For example, what if you are an employee of the company? What if you are a neighboring landowner who just happened to overhear some workers discussing the ore strike? What if your brother works for the company and he told you about the ore strike?

_____

_____

_____

_____

_____

4. Is Insider Trading Wrong? As the preceding makes clear, the law treats securities differently than it does other assets. Can you think of reasons why this is so? Does this differing treatment make sense? After all, is insider trading even wrong? *See* Alan Studler and Eric W. Orts, *Moral Principles in the Law of Insider Trading*, 78 TEX. L. REV. 375 (1999); *Leviticus* 6:1-5, 19:35-36; *Deuteronomy* 25:13-16; *Proverbs* 11:1, 16:11, 20:10, 20:23; *Ezekiel* 45:10; and *Micah* 6:11-12.

_____

_____

_____

_____

_____

5. Should it be Punishable by the Civil Government? Not every instance of wrongdoing is punishable by the civil government. For example, if I promise my wife to take the trash out and forget to do it, I have committed a sin. However, one would assume that there is no role for the sheriff in this situation.

Assuming that insider trading is wrong, should it be within the role of the civil government to punish it? *See Romans* 13:1-7; 1 *Peter* 2:13-17; Roger Bern, *A Biblical Model for Analysis of Issues of Law and Public*

Policy: with Illustrative Applications to Contracts, Antitrust, Remedies and Public Policy Issues, 6 REGENT U. L. REV. 103, 116-131 (1995).

_____

_____

_____

_____

_____

_____

6. Political Insider Trading? Should members of Congress be able to trade securities based upon nonpublic information that they have access to through their positions in Congress? As this book goes to press, "political insider trading" of this kind is a breaking scandal. *See 60 Minutes: Insiders* (CBS television broadcast Nov. 13, 2011); *Congress: Trading Stock on Inside Information?*, CBS NEWS (Nov. 13, 2011, 7:06 PM), http://www.cbsnews.com/8301-18560_162-57323527/congress-trading-stock-on-inside-information; and Brody Mullins, *Congress Pushing Curb on Trading*, WALL ST. J., Dec. 6, 2011, http://online.wsj.com/article/SB10001424052970204083204577082751846890664.html.

_____

_____

_____

_____

_____

_____

INDEX